*What Others Are Saying:*

I am so pleased with Peter Hill's work in this area and his intense study (both in the scriptures and in life applications) to address this subject from a unique point of view. The Holy Spirit will speak to you clearly as you read the pages of this book and help you understand the different elements that are involved in living a life acceptable unto God. I advise all Christians everywhere to read this book. The Body of Christ needs to have such a read.

~ *Glen Stead, President, CFCM*

A Biblical, relevant, balanced and insightful word on the subject of purity, as well as a helpful guide for those wanting to avoid legalism and license and walk the path of liberty we have in Christ. Most powerful however, is that Peter speaks from his own experience and lives what he teaches.

~ *Dr Henry Schorr, Senior Pastor, Centre Street Church*

In a world where there seems to be little concern for purity and integrity, Peter Hill offers a book that explores these topics through the lens of our reasonable worship of Jesus, the Object of our devotion. The Process of Purity explores the reality of purity being something which Jesus does in us more than what we do in and of our own efforts. Peter wonderfully weaves in personal reflections with scriptural examination to encourage the reader that purity is a choice we allow Jesus to work in us. Our sacrifice—our reasonable worship—is being willing to climb onto the altar, starving the sinful nature and remaining malleable in the Master's hands. I commend this book—Peter's labour of love—to you, not so much as a guide book to purity as an encouragement to whole-hearted, life-giving reasonable worship.

~ *Gareth Goossen, Executive Director, Make Us Holy Ministries*

This book is a must-read for a generation who is in the 'process'. Peter shares his journey and offers a biblical foundation for freedom in Christ. Read this book slowly—allow the stories, scriptures and encouragement to penetrate deep—and rely on the Holy Spirit to break the chains that hold you. I believe you will be encouraged as you pursue Him.

*~ Tim MacDonald, Vice Chairman, CPM Enterprises*

The Process of Purity—relevant, Biblically insightful, and most of all real. Share the life changing experiences with Peter Hill. Understand the challenges to those who desire purity as a way of life. This is a book with a message to those who desire more than a normal life. "Blessed are the pure in heart, for they shall see God" (Matthew 5:8).

*~ Len Zoeteman, Vice President, CFCM*

# The Process of Purity

### Living Our Lives as a Reasonable Act of Worship

**PETER HILL**

CPM Publications
Calgary, AB, Canada
cpm-e.com

The Process of Purity: Living Our Lives as a Reasonable Act of Worship
© 2008 Peter Hill

ISBN-10: 1-897373-54-6
ISBN-13: 978-1-897373-54-5

All rights reserved. No portion of this book may be reproduced, stored in a retrieval system, or transmitted in any form or by any means—electronic, mechanical, photocopy, recording, or any other—except for brief quotations in printed reviews, without the prior permission of the publisher.

Published work owned and operated by CPM Publications, a division of CPM Enterprises, Calgary, AB.

Printed by Word Alive Press, Winnipeg, MB. (www.wordalivepress.ca)

Unless otherwise indicated, all Scripture quotations are taken from the *Holy Bible*, New Living Translation, copyright © 1996. Used by permission of Tyndale House Publishers, Inc., Wheaton, Illinois 60189. All rights reserved.

Other Scripture references are from the following sources.

THE AMPLIFIED BIBLE (AMP), Copyright © 1954, 1958, 1962, 1964, 1965, 1987 by the Lockman Foundation. All rights reserved. Used by permission. (www.Lockman.org). THE MESSAGE (MSG). Copyright © by Eugene H. Peterson 1993, 1994, 1995, 1996, 2000, 2001, 2002. Used by permission of NavPress Publishing Group. The HOLY BIBLE, NEW INTERNATIONAL VERSION (NIV). Copyright © 1973, 1978, 1984 International Bible Society. Used by permission of Zondervan Bible Publishers. The New King James Version (NKJV). Copyright © 1979, 1980, 1982, Thomas Nelson, Inc., Publishers.

In quoting Scripture, the letter "a" has been used to denote the first portion of a cited reference, while the letter "b" has been used to denote a quote from the last portion.

Author's Note: Some of the anecdotal illustrations, although true to life, have been altered to protect the privacy of the persons involved. Other illustrations are fictional, and any resemblance to people living or dead is coincidental.

*To Danielle*
*Your hand in mine...*
*Who could ask for anything more?*

# Table of Contents:

Acknowledgements: ix
Introduction: xi

Part 1: A Starting Ground   1

    Chapter 1: Our Reasonable Act of Worship   3
    Chapter 2: Looking in the Mirror   11
    Chapter 3: Sincerity of Approach   23
    Chapter 4: Understanding Devotion   35

Part 2: A Battleground   47

    Chapter 5: A Confusing Situation   49
    Chapter 6: Living Sacrifice   63
    Chapter 7: Captive Thoughts   77
    Chapter 8: Exterior Battle Lines   91
    Chapter 9: The Battle Continues   109

Part 3: Standing on Firm Ground   127

    Chapter 10: Heart Transplant   129
    Chapter 11: Ponderings for the Passage   145
    Chapter 12: Are We There Yet?   159

Endnotes:   171

# Acknowledgements:

Projects like this simply don't happen without a team of people behind you. I cannot begin this book properly without taking the time to thank so many who have helped, supported, and encouraged me to see this project through to its entirety. We are not an island unto ourselves, and I am so thankful to be able to share my gratitude with the following people:

*Danielle*—your smile lights up a room, and your glance lights up my heart. I am so thankful that God has united the two of us together. To have you by my side is a greater joy than any man could fathom. You will forever be my princess, and I will be eternally grateful.

*Mom and Dad*—they say you can't pick the family you get. I am incredibly blessed that God decided to place me where he did. I am so grateful for the example both of you have been and continue to be to me. God will keep on using you in all that you do, and he will honour you for the servant's heart that you've each been faithful to carry. The journey's only just begun.

*CPM's Board of Directors*—Danielle and I are so thankful to have a team of people behind this business that we can consider our friends. Thank you for your support, your belief in us, your encouragement, and your grace along the way. We treasure you.

*My Editing Team*—so many people have been willing to sit down with their red (or green, or purple) pens and hash through my thoughts. Thank you to all of you. You have brought life to confusion, and clarity to my made-up dictionary. I think the greatest thing that came out of the editing process was the conversations...thanks for those as well.

*Tim MacDonald*—you seem to wear so many hats when it comes to our relationship...my pastor, my advisor, my vice chairman, and my business partner. The one I value the most, though, is my friend. Thanks for your continued support. We are praying that doors continue to open for you.

*Henry Schorr*—I am blessed to attend a church with you at the helm. Thanks for taking the time to believe in me and in this project. May God continue to bless you.

*Len Zoeteman*—reproducibility. God was able to birth something in me years ago because you were willing to be used as his spokesperson. You are a true apostle. Thank you. I value the time we spend together and the relationship we have.

*Glen Stead*—our nation is crying out for leaders who are willing to finish well. You have been faithful to pour yourself into the next generation of spiritual leaders. I am grateful for your servant's heart. Thanks for supporting me in this project.

*Gareth Goossen*—it's funny how God can weave the paths of two strangers together. I am thankful our paths crossed years ago. I believe in you and the work you are doing. God's hand is upon you. Great things are in store.

# Introduction:

To hell in a hand basket.

Ask the common person on your neighbourhood street corner where they think our world is headed, and this is proclaimed as the most widespread answer. It seems to be the general consensus of everyone you meet, a common viewpoint of both the inexperienced and the sage. It is a philosophy that tries to force its way to the forefront in even the most faith-filled Christian. Why? Because our world seems to be spinning out of control and into utter chaos.

Take a walk downtown in the community you call home and you'll inevitably see it: the latest sex toy, the newest drug, the hidden stock that's about to go public and win you your retirement. We are bombarded with stuff trying to fulfill us. We are inundated with replacements for a love that we all innately crave.

The problem with counterfeits? None of them work. Need proof? Just watch the news. Pastors fall from their high posts because of a secret drug addition that comes to the attention of the media. TV evangelists descend from the watchful public eye because of a life intertwined with sex and scandal. The guy next door suddenly decides his wife no longer means anything to him and his commitment is no longer required, abandoning his vows in lieu of some temporary fix for his mid-life crisis.

Deep within the heart of each one of us there is a cry for something more. If we are honest with ourselves, our answer to where this world is headed is too often the same...going to hell in a hand basket. And the rate of travel seems to be getting quicker.

I was riding the train home from a conference in the downtown core of my city when a couple in their late thirties entered the car I was in. Their entrance immediately changed the atmosphere. Maybe my sensitivity was heightened at that moment because God and I were already in the middle of a conversation, but I knew there was a tangible distress in the lives of these two individuals. The tension I could feel in the air was all I needed for validation. They soon came over and sat behind me. My nose caught the all too familiar smell of Listerine that tries to hide intoxication and cheap cigarettes.

My heart bled for the couple as I listened to them. She was crying. His speech was slurred. For a moment, my mind was consumed with their lives instead of my own. What were their fears? What were their hopes? What were their regrets? I watched them and listened, wondering if they knew there was hope. I began to look around the train at the faces of all the people I saw. Each face represented a different life, a different story, a different struggle. Each face was longing to feel fulfilled and loved. Each face was crying out for something different than what this world has to offer.

My eyes were opened to the lives of others and I suddenly felt incredibly small. I was one person on one train in one city. I began to think about just how big this world really is. How can any one of us have any real significance in this world? How can any one of us make a difference in the lives of so many hurting people?

What can I do in a world that is so out of control?

In the middle of millions, I have significance. So do you. What you do with that significance is ultimately up to you.

> *Whom should I send as a messenger to my people? Who will go for us?*
>
> *~ Isaiah 6:8b*

Within the centre of the chaos, God calls us to something different. God calls us to something unique. We so easily get caught up in the fast-paced travel of this world. We blend in with insignificance and are blinded to the world around us.

>Where do I fit?
>Why do I matter?
>What can I do?

If you are honest with yourself, these thoughts infiltrate your mind. You are just one person in the middle of it all. God told Abraham his children would be as numerous as the grains of sand. How can one grain ever have meaning in a sea of broken rocks? How can you ever hope to change things? Why even bother?

May I suggest a different approach?

God is not asking you to change the world—he is asking you to change yourself. Your life of purity is the ultimate call that God has placed on your life. Living out his ideals in an idealistic world is what this journey is all about, and I pray that this book will help you see that journey.

I believe that a person's spiritual walk is a continual process. Perhaps the packaging of this book is a little different from the packaging of another, but the message is the same because the message has not changed for over 2000 years. The more we get the message into our small-minded and mortal brains, the more we can live out this process of purity in our daily lives.

I teach math at a high school in my city. One of the things we do a lot of in my classroom is word problems, or scenario based questions. Time and time again I remind my students to show their work. The message I send to them on a daily basis is that their answer to a question is never as important as their course of arrival. The process is always more important than the product.

I believe that in life it is the same thing. In reality, we are not going to be completely pure beings while we continue to breathe the oxygen that is on this earth. Purity is going to involve a battle we face every second of every day until we leave our earthly bodies. We often encounter forks in the road called life that give us a choice of two paths. Sometimes we choose the path of purity, sometimes we don't.

Sometimes we take the low road. Then we beat ourselves up over the mistakes that we have made when all God is asking is that we pick ourselves up and try again. Sometimes we take the high road, only to face fork after fork. We get overwhelmed with the choices and give in to the complacency of believing we will never make it. We end up wondering why we even bother to try.

I want to deal with both of these paths throughout this book because I have come to see just how dangerous they both can be. Maybe we have missed the point altogether. Maybe God is never as concerned with the product of purity as he is with the process of purity. Living out the process means picking ourselves up when we fall and not giving up when faced with the same battle again.

This is where the title of the book you're holding comes from. The key to a successful and fulfilled life here on earth is the *process* of living pure. As you can see, if you took the time to read the table of contents, I have separated this book into three sections. The first section is meant to give us a starting ground—where we want to go and what we need to know. The second section deals with some of the nitty gritty—the, 'fleshing it out in the reality of the world we live in' stuff. The last section looks at how to sustain this process of purity. Once we have established the battle lines and boundary posts to help us live it out, there are other hurdles to overcome within the process.

This book is not meant to be a quick read. Please take your time and let each chapter sink in. I am in no rush, nor should you be. To help you get the most out of the pages before you, we have also provided an online study guide that can be printed. There are spots for you to journal through your journey, as well as reflective questions that are ideal for yourself or for your small group. This online journal is available to you for free from our website, cpm-e.com.

So begins the process of this book. So begins the process of purity for my life and I hope for yours. I am excited to journey with you, for this book will be as much about my own journey as it will be about yours. We're all in this together. God did not create us to live in isolation or seclusion, so let's stand together, read together, and journey together.

I labour...in what follows, [because] my efforts to be clear...may suggest a confidence which I by no means feel. I should be mad if I did. Take it as one man's reverie....If anything in it is useful to you, use it; if anything is not, never give it a second thought.

~ C. S. Lewis[1]

# Part 1:
# A Starting Ground

You placed the world on its foundation so it would never be moved.

~Psalm 104:5

By doing this they will be storing up their treasure as a good foundation for the future so that they may take hold of real life.

~1 Timothy 6:19

# Chapter 1: Our Reasonable Act of Worship

Therefore, I urge you, brothers, in view of God's mercy, to offer your bodies as living sacrifices, holy and pleasing to God—this is your spiritual act of worship. Do not conform any longer to the pattern of this world, but be transformed by the renewing of your mind. Then you will be able to test and approve what God's will is—his good, pleasing and perfect will.

~Romans 12:1–2 (NIV)

I consider myself to be a reasonable man.

OK, maybe a little high strung from time to time, but reasonable nonetheless. I don't fly off the handle too quickly. I listen to both sides of the story and turn my lights off when I am not using them. I don't litter, although I do have a nasty habit of spitting my gum out on the ground. I bite my tongue when it's not my place to speak and I try not to offend my brother. I give of my tithes, my time, and my taxes. I wash behind my ears and make sure my underwear is clean before getting into a car accident.

These are all reasonable things to do in our society, so it seems fitting that I would be considered a reasonable man. Call me Practical Peter and call yourself Levelheaded Leon. Maybe you are Rational Rachael or Sound Sally.

We are, for the most part, sensible beings who do reasonable things. Of course, to be a reasonable person begs the question of what it all is supposed to look like.

What does it mean to be reasonable?

If we take a quick look in the dictionary, we find definitions like 'being in accordance with reason' or 'having sound judgment'. Check out your local paperback thesaurus and you find synonyms like rational, logical, evenhanded, and sensible. To be reasonable is to do the right thing or to give a fair assessment. The reasonable man considers all facts, weighs all options, and takes the optimal course of action.

The verse we started this chapter with serves as both the beginning and the end of our journey. Let your eyes wander back for another read through. Meditate on it for a moment or two. Linger on the words and their meaning. Perhaps I should call it the 'Romans 1-2 Punch', since I am so into sports analogies (you'll catch my sarcasm soon). Either way, it is going to form the basis for and the reasoning behind this entire collection of thoughts, tangents, and testimonies that I am now calling a book.

The word 'spiritual' in the end of verse 1 can also be translated as 'reasonable'. This offering of ourselves as living sacrifices, this process of purity that we want to unpack and unfold, is really what our life calling is all about. If God has created us to worship him in spirit and in truth, living a life of purity becomes our reasonable act of worship.

God is not looking for us first and foremost to evangelize. His sole purpose in leaving us on this earth is not to care for the sick, to help the poor, or even to preach the good news. First and foremost, he is looking for people who are willing to live for him. He is looking for people who are willing to worship with abandon, who are willing to mount their own altars and sacrifice their lives on a daily basis. He is looking for people who realize that their God is more important than anything else in their lives.

> **God is looking for people who are willing to live for him...who are willing to worship with abandon.**

When we truly see him, we begin to realize that
offering our entire selves to him is really
the only reasonable thing to do.

Above all, we need to understand the command. God is looking for people who are willing to present themselves—not their talents, their money, or their time, but their entire beings—to him in spiritual worship. God is looking for people who are willing to have their minds transformed. God is looking for people who are willing to live out the process of purity as their reasonable act of worship.

## THE THREE PURITIES...

If we are to live out this process of purity, we need to look a little more closely at what exactly we mean by the word purity. What does living a pure life look like? Does it mean I don't have sex before marriage? Does it mean I remain faithful to my spouse in body and in mind? For sure it does, but it means much more than that as well. Really, when we think about the word purity, we often think of only one kind of purity, that of sexual purity— honouring God with our bodies.

In a lot of ways, this is the purity issue we struggle with the most, regardless of whether we are male or female. There is so much to cover with regards to sexual purity that many books have been written on this one subject alone. Yet, if we take a step back and look at a slightly bigger picture, there are really three main areas of living a pure life. These are the areas we need to develop if we want to live out this process as our reasonable act of worship. We can get our cue from the Apostle John's first letter to the Gentile churches.

> *Stop loving this evil world and all that it offers you, for when you love the world, you show that you do not have the love of the Father in you. For the world offers only the lust for physical pleasure, the lust for everything we see, and pride in our possessions. These are not from the*

> Father. They are from this evil world. And this world is fading away, along with everything it craves. But if you do the will of God, you will live forever.
>
> ~ 1 John 2:15-17

The first area John outlines is the lust for physical pleasure. Included here is a lust for things of a sexual nature, but this particular shopping list is a little longer than just one item. Anything that gives our body physical pleasure is included in this list. So we had better add gluttony and perhaps alcohol abuse. The list can be lengthy, but the root issues are the same. We try to meet our needs for physical pleasure outside of the boundaries God has given us.

**Purity Areas:**
- Lust for physical pleasure
- Lust for everything we see
- Pride in our possessions

The second area that John talks about is the lust for everything we see. We have all bowed to the idol of materialism at one point or another. We feel the need to have the latest toys, the fastest computers, and the newest cars. Whether we are a have or a have not, we want what we don't have and have what we don't want. We get caught in the, 'I'd be happy if' syndrome: I'd be happy if I could just have that newer house, that shinier car, that younger wife. The 'toy temptation' is a constant struggle.

Finally, the third area of purity involves pride in our possessions. This may sound similar to the second, but you need to dig a little deeper. The battle we face here is one of pride in ourselves. The Amplified version talks of "the pride of life [assurance in one's own resources or in the stability of earthly things]" (v. 16). It is the self-assured and boastful attitude that is displayed by so many of us. It's the 'I can do it on my own' mentality that is the reason for so many stumbles in this process of purity we are walking through.

These three areas of purity are satan's main attack. In reality, satan has not really come up with anything new since he was kicked out of heaven. Rather, he ends up repacking the same lies and stories to fit each historical era. Heading back to the beginning of time and the account of creation, we can read about the same three purity issues in the Garden of Eden (see Genesis 3:1-6).

We also see a parallel in the temptations of Jesus while he was wrapped in flesh and within the boundaries of a human mind. Check out Matthew 4 for the full wilderness account. Jesus was tempted in the area of physical purity by the suggestion he turn stones into bread. He had to resist materialism by being offered the kingdoms of the world. In the area of pride in one's own resources, Jesus was tempted to jump off a Jerusalem high-rise to prove he was the protected Son of God.

The difference between Jesus' process of purity and our own? He made it through successfully the first time around! In fact, the Bible says he knew no sin.

> *That is why we have a great High Priest who has gone to heaven, Jesus the Son of God. Let us cling to him and never stop trusting him. This High Priest of ours understands our weaknesses, for he faced all of the same temptations we do, yet he did not sin. So let us come boldly to the throne of our gracious God. There we will receive his mercy, and we will find grace to help us when we need it.*
> ~ *Hebrews 4:14-16*

Jesus has given us the example of purity to follow. Are we living it fully? I doubt if any of us could say we have maxed out on our potential for pure living. But this is the template that has been given to us, and this is the process that we must walk through. When all is said and done and we have breathed our last breath, our journey will be over and our journey will be evaluated. We each have a yearning in our heart for that evaluation to bring forth one result—those eternal words that have been implanted deep inside each one of us...

> *Well done, my good and faithful servant. You have been faithful....Let's celebrate together!*
> ~ *Matthew 25:21b*

Well done. At the end of the day, that is what it comes down to—for the immortal and invisible, the all-powerful and all-knowing creator of the universe to look deep into our eyes, to smile at us, and to say well done. This is what we are living for. This is why we are on this journey together. May it be said of each one of us that we journeyed through this process of purity to the best of our ability.

# Chapter 2: Looking in the Mirror

Blessed are the pure in heart, for they shall see God.

~Matthew 5:8 (NKJV)

A mirror is a funny thing. We live in a world where we seem to be obsessed with ourselves. We are fascinated by our image—that outward surface reflection of our being. One of the last things a person does before walking out the door is to look themselves over in the mirror. It's imperative they make sure their hair is okay, their teeth are clean, and that all zits on their forehead have been popped.

We want to make the right first impression on the people we come in contact with, so we vainly check and recheck ourselves to make certain we are coming across the way we want to. Look around you the next time you stop at a red light and you'll see what I mean. I don't believe rear-view mirrors were ever invented to check out what's behind you. They rather seem to be ingenious tools for making sure there are no poppy seeds stuck between your teeth after that spinach salad you had for dinner.

When we look in the mirror, however, we only look at our features. Seldom do we look at ourselves. The closest thing one gets to eye contact becomes the woman putting on mascara at that momentary pause in her commute to work.

We check our features, but we don't check ourselves. Why is that? Perhaps, if we are

**We check our features, but we don't check ourselves.**

completely honest with ourselves, we don't really like the image looking back at us. The successful business entrepreneur avoids eye contact with himself because he sees the people he pounced on during his climb to the top. The devoted preacher avoids observing his eyes in the mirror because they speak of a family he has neglected for a ministry that he covets.

The fact is, for as much time as we do spend in the mirror, we tend not to like to look at ourselves. We look at the outside, but seldom do we allow ourselves to peel away some of those superficial layers and look beyond the skin and bones. If we are to begin this process of living our lives as a reasonable act of worship, I believe this is the first step along the journey. We need to stop and take a hard look at ourselves in a mirror. We need to begin with an inventory of the person who is staring back at us.

> We need to first be willing
> to see ourselves as God sees us.

## IF YOU COULD SEE...

Integrity is one of those words that gets bounced around in Christian and secular circles alike. We long for it in our own lives; we search for it in the lives of others; and very often, we come up short in both the former and the latter.

I want to be a man of integrity. I want people to remember me as one who exhibited a strong character and a godly nature. This is the legacy I believe we all want to leave.

The fact of the matter is that I often feel like I have a long road ahead of me if I am ever going to reach that point. I am torn between the spiritual me (which is the one I try to show the most) and the not-so-spiritual me—the one who battles and fails, lies and cheats, weasels and worms. There seems to be a constant disconnect between the guy I want to be and the guy I usually end up being.

I don't feel like I have a whole lot of character. In fact, I feel more like satan's worm than God's child at times. I find myself wondering if my life is ever going to be fixed. I wonder if I am ever going to be able to stand up for my own values, to be the man that I want to be.

By the way, I am not saying any of this for your sympathy. Rather, I am telling you this because I have a sneaky suspicion that you feel the same. Why we feel the need to mask ourselves and pretend we have it all together, I will never understand. It's like going to a wart clinic and trying to pretend with everyone in the waiting room that you don't have a wart.

Living our lives as a process of purity involves becoming men and women of integrity. Take a look in that mirror—do you see a person of integrity? Or do you feel your reflection is more like the worm I have already described?

> We feel the need to mask ourselves and pretend we have it all together. Instead, God is looking for integrity.

Pick up a dictionary and it will define integrity as the firm adherence to a code of especially moral or artistic values; the quality or state of being complete or undivided.² James encourages us to be undivided in our minds, lest we be "as unsettled as a wave of the sea that is driven and tossed by the wind. People like that should not expect to receive anything from the Lord" (James 1:6-7).

> A life that is undivided.
> Is that what I am living?
> Is that the character that I am portraying?

What does it look like? Therein lies the problem, I think. We often cannot see what it looks like because we are too caught up in our own dividedness to picture what an undivided life might be. We run away from Christ instead of running toward him. We cannot see beyond our cloud of brokenness. We cannot see beyond our shrouds of shame. We cannot see beyond ourselves.

If only we could see.

If we could see what Christ sees when he looks at us, maybe we could begin to move away from our dividedness. Maybe we could begin to calm our restless heart and start living the life of integrity that each of us longs to live. If we could see what Christ sees, maybe we would have the strength to not pick up that bottle for the thousandth 'last time', to not raise our hand against our wife or our children, to not lie or manipulate ourselves out of a transparent situation. If we could see that Christ has not given up on us, perhaps we could gather up just that last bit of strength needed to not give up on ourselves.

If only we could see.

Strip it all away...the clothes, the career, the ministry, the family, the accomplishments. What are you left with? What do you see in that mirror? A broken, messed up life.

See beyond your sin.

That temper that flared up again? That addiction you gave in to instead of running from? That altar you stepped down from instead of sacrificing yourself upon? Maybe if we began to see what God sees, the impurities in our lives would no longer be an issue. Maybe the reason we have not gained victory in those aspects of our lives is that our vision does not go beyond our failures. Until we begin to see beyond our sin there is no way God can help us conquer it.

See beyond your accomplishments.

Do you remember that mountaintop experience you had long ago? Do you remember that time when it seemed like God was working so clearly through you? Remember how you felt so in tune with his spirit? Are you wondering why you can't return to that place? Perhaps it is because you are living in the light of past accomplishments instead of future glory. Perhaps God is trying to do a new thing in you but you are so focused on what he has done in the past that you cannot see what he is trying to do in your future. It's good to remember what God has accomplished through us, but we cannot stay there lest our pride give way to self indulgence and bitterness. We need to look beyond what God has done and toward what he still wants to do.

See beyond yourself.

Geoff Moore penned these words in a song for his wife a few years ago.

*And you would know you have my heart*
*If you could see what I see*
*That a treasure's what you are*
*If you could see what I see...*
*If beauty is all in the eye of the beholder*
*Then I am beholding true beauty*[3]

When I was a teenager, I always said that would be the song I sang to my wife on our wedding day. It turns out that it was! Lately, though, it's being sung back to me. God has been gently singing it to me when I have been too embarrassed to come close to him. He has been softly singing when I have been too proud to be honest. This is God's heart; this is God's desire—that you and I see what he sees.

Part 1: A Starting Ground

> Integrity comes through a person who is able to look in the mirror through a lens of perfect justice combined with divine mercy. Integrity begins when we begin to see what God sees.

Am I a man of integrity? I guess if you look in the natural realm it all depends on the day. But this one thing I know—integrity comes from within a person who is willing to see past their barriers and hang ups. Integrity comes through a person who is able to look in the mirror through a lens of perfect justice combined with divine mercy. Integrity begins when we begin to see what God sees.

## OPEN EYES AND PURE HEARTS...

The desire for integrity is within each one of us. The craving to live in such a relationship with our creator—that we see what he sees—runs deep within the canyons of our souls. We cry out with the psalmist, "God, open my eyes that I may see!" (see Psalm 119:18). We long to see the face of the Lord, to gaze upon his countenance. Like Moses, we plead, "Show me your glory!" (see Exodus 33:18). We long to see God move in our lives in a way he has never moved before. But sometimes we miss a verse...

> *Blessed are the pure in heart, for they shall see God.*
> *~ Matthew 5:8 (NKJV)*

How is your visibility today? What is the state of your heart? I am beginning to see how these two questions are one and the same. It is those who are pure in heart that will see God move. When I think about these issues of living a pure life—what it means to offer myself as a living sacrifice for my reasonable act of worship—I always gain some hope from King David in the Old Testament.

Within the pages of the Bible, King David was called a man after God's own heart.[4] Yet when we dig into the pages of recorded Biblical history, we see a picture of a man who doesn't always reflect this calling. King David could have been remembered as a thief, a liar, a cheater, a voyeur, an adulterer, and even a murderer. He was a man who let his fantasies run out of control and suffered severe consequences as a result.

> How is your visibility today? What is the state of your heart? These two questions are one and the same.

But it was also David who longed for purity. It was David who was willing to stand without a mask before his creator and ask to have his innermost thoughts searched (see Psalm 139:23). It was this willingness that also allowed David to know the power of repentance and forgiveness (see Psalm 51). David knew the importance of discipline, of consistency, and of getting back up when he fell off the wagon. Take a moment to read Psalm 101 and you will see the heart of someone determined to live with integrity. Browse through many other Psalms written by this shepherd-turned-king and you will catch a reflective glimpse of someone willing to take an honest look at himself in the mirror. You will also see someone who was willing to do something about the reflection looking back at him.

What about you? Are you willing to work at it? Are you willing to begin consistently renewing your mind by the cleansing of the word (see Ephesians 5:26)? It is through the study of scripture that our minds are transformed and our sight restored.

*How can a young person live a clean life?*
*By carefully reading the map of your Word.*

> *I'm single-minded in pursuit of you;*
> *don't let me miss the road signs you've posted.*
> ~ Psalm 119:9-10 (MSG)

How strong is your desire to see the face of God reflected in your own face? Are you single-minded in your pursuit? How willing are you to become the person he sees through his eyes?

We need to realize the importance of the process. Having a pure heart does not involve how many times you have fallen down—only that you've picked yourself back up again. The focal point of our journey of purity needs to shift to the process—the daily consistency, the daily discipline, the daily hiding of the word in our hearts that we might not sin (see Psalm 119:11).

God is not looking for perfection; he's looking for people who are willing to take an honest look in the mirror and begin to take stock of their lives—to look at what needs to be worked on and what needs to be developed. God is looking for people who are willing to walk through the process. A person who is able to gratefully accept the victories along the way and not allow defeats to cause an endless stumble is what he longs for. Yet we tolerate so many other things in our lives that vie for our attention. We get busy, we let our consistency slide, and we suddenly wonder why we can't see God anymore.

> Open my eyes that I may see...
> Search me, O God, and know my thoughts...

Let's show God that we, like David, are indeed after his heart. Let's show God that we are willing to walk through the process.

Let's show God that we are serious. The implications of people willing to do this are earth-changing and history-making.

There is a lot of unpacking to do here. Let's not rush this moment. Living out our lives in purity is an attainable reality. It is a reality that you will see step-by-step and chapter-by-chapter. Take a minute, put the book down and go for a walk. Find a mirror and take a good long look—not at your features, but at your soul. Be willing to take inventory. In your personal time of devotions and scripture reading, allow God to show you what he sees. Trust him to show you the areas he wants to begin working on.

> Let's show God that we are indeed after his heart. Let's show God that we are serious.

Don't be afraid—God will be with you every step of the way. Let him do the work inside that both of you are longing for. Look deeper—go past the face and behind the mask. Be willing to be vulnerable and look at yourself through his eyes. Sure, you're a little rough around the edges, but you are still his masterpiece.

# Chapter 3: Sincerity of Approach

Love must be sincere. Hate what is evil; cling to what is good. Be devoted to one another in brotherly love. Honor one another above yourselves.

~Romans 12:9-10 (NIV)

We are called to live this life—to walk through this process of purity—with sincere hearts. I think many of us struggle with what that actually looks like in a world where sincerity is not always commonplace. Instead, we get immersed inside the rat race of life...quick smiles and tipped hats as we pass each other by. We politely nod and ask how the other is doing without really expecting an answer other than, "Fine, and you?" Obtaining the superficial response, we continue on our merry way, the conversation forced to end by this time because no one stopped and both parties are now out of earshot.

God calls us to something different. God calls us, as Paul states in the verse we opened this chapter with, to live life with a love that is sincere. Let's read the same verse in *The Message* translation by Eugene Peterson...

> *Love from the center of who you are; don't fake it. Run for dear life from evil; hold on for dear life to good. Be good friends who love deeply; practice playing second fiddle.*

It is said that you have two choices in living your life. You can pour all of your time and energy into tearing down the door that seems to stand in your way, or you can find a key, unlock the door, and walk through. I believe that as we begin to obtain the keys for some of these things in our lives, our walk through the process of purity becomes much more manageable. I find Peterson's translation of this verse interesting. Could it be that the key to approaching life with sincerity is the same key that allows you to enjoy playing second fiddle?

## SINCERELY YOURS...

Modern technology is a wonderful thing. I can sit at my desk and type a letter on a computer that practically reads my thoughts. As I stare at the screen and begin to type out the date, a little box appears. The computer, in its infinite wisdom and knowledge, has determined I am typing the date and allows me to have the entire chronological stamp appear simply by pressing the enter key. How did my buddy Bill ever think of that?

> You can pour all of your time and energy into tearing down the door that seems to stand in your way, or you can find a key and unlock the door.

As I come to the close of my little letter, another option box appears with the following phrase...

Sincerely Yours,

Sincerely yours. It's a common ending for a formal note of correspondence. It has appeared on countless proposals, limitless propositions, and incalculable postings. It has been penned by the business man who is anxious to seal that next deal and collect his revenue. It has been crafted by the soldier captured by the love of his life but haunted by the miles between them.

What does 'sincere' mean? What does the word 'sincere' imply? Interestingly enough, Webster's answers those questions not by telling us what it is, but rather, by saying what is missing. It is the "absence of hypocrisy," "the absence of pretend," "the absence of embellishment and exaggeration."[5] It's unadulterated honesty...vulnerable realness of one person toward another. In many ways, it's something superficially said but not deeply seen in today's world. Yet it is the heart cry of the one who spoke the world into existence.

King David heard this heart cry and learned the value of being sincere after a mask he was trying to wear caught up with him. We have already mentioned that this man after God's own heart had a few stumbles along the way. One of his more infamous missteps was a rendezvous with forbidden fruit and a bloodshed cover up that followed. Take a minute and read through 2 Samuel 11-12 for the full account.

> Sincerity is unadulterated honesty, vulnerable realness, and the heart cry of the one who spoke the world into existence.

When the dust settles and this mighty leader checks out the sacrificial list for the atonement of his particular grievances, he comes up short. There is no lamb that will meet the qualifications for reversing adultery and no goat's blood to take care of murder. In fact, Levitical law stated that the judgment for either act was death (see Leviticus 20:10; 24:17).

David hit a wall. He came to the point where a ritualistic sacrifice would not cut it anymore. That's when he discovered something. David was given a divine foretaste of things to come—a celestial sample of what we now live in. It was not the animal sacrifice God really cared about. It was not the ritual he was concerned with, but rather, the heart of the person making the sacrifice. God looked for a heart of sincerity over that of shallow motions and artificial rites. David penned these words after Nathan confronted him about his sin:

> *You would not be pleased with sacrifices, or I would bring them.*

*Part 1: A Starting Ground*

> *If I brought you a burnt offering, you would not accept it.*
> *The sacrifice you want is a broken spirit.*
> *A broken and repentant heart, O God, you will not despise.*
>
> ~Psalm 51:16-17

David realized that God longed for the sacrifice of a sincere heart. It was David's honest approach that allowed him to work out his process of purity in the middle of a few wrong turns. Today, it is still the sincerity of approach that God longs for.

> *Let us draw near to God with a sincere heart in full assurance of faith, having our hearts sprinkled to cleanse us from a guilty conscience and having our bodies washed with pure water.*
>
> ~Hebrews 10:22 (NIV)

Does sincerity mean that you come to God with everything all together? Quite the opposite is true. Coming to God with a sincere heart is approaching him in humility and being willing to talk with him about the dark areas of your life instead of trying to pretend that they aren't there or aren't important.

Sincerity is to approach God without a mask. It is this sacrifice that he loves. He delights in your vulnerability, for it opens the door for his cleansing atonement to come and wash you. It welcomes him to enter into those forbidden places of your heart and clean them out. God won't come if he's not invited. It is the sincerity, the honesty, the lack of pretentiousness that allows him

> **Sincerity is to approach God without a mask. He delights in your vulnerability, for it opens the door and welcomes him into those forbidden places of your heart.**

the entry into your life he so deeply desires. It is in the sincerity of our approach that God is given permission to help us walk through this process of purity.

David was able to approach the throne of God with a clean conscience because he came with a sincere heart. There is power in that. We are able to approach God in the same way. When we come stripped of our own pride and self-importance, our hearts can be cleansed and our worship can be true.

So, how about it? Are you ready to approach God with the sacrifice of a sincere heart? Are you ready to be real with the one who knows everything about you?

## Bogotá or Bust...

We need to approach God with a heart that is sincere, but I believe that is only door number one. Living a life of purity also involves approaching our fellow man with a heart of sincerity. If God was only concerned with how we approached him, I doubt he would have left us on this earth once we devoted our lives to him for eternity. I think God is interested in the interpersonal relationships we have just as much as in the relationship we have with him.

God longs for you to genuinely ask someone how they are doing and then to take the time to listen to their response. I think, deep down, you long for the same. God has created us with a desire for sincerity and it's time we allowed that desire to come back up to the surface of our lives. Perhaps it's time we practiced playing a little more second fiddle.

I am not a person who believes all menial tasks must be directly inspired from above. I don't ask God whether or not this is the proper time for me to brush my teeth or to get up and go to work—these are just parts of everyday life. That being said, I believe we evangelicals have lost some of the wonder of seeing the divine interspersed with the mundane.

When he wrapped himself in human skin, Jesus operated with a heart of sincerity toward his heavenly Father and toward his fellow man. As we are called to do the same, we should take a close look at the model he left for us to follow.

Let me share a story...

> **Jesus operated with a heart of sincerity toward his Father and toward his fellow man. We are called to do the same.**

I was en route to Trinidad & Tobago to visit with close friends. As I boarded the plane in Calgary, the lady in front of me was having trouble getting her bag into the overhead bin. I smiled, took it from her, and got it situated in the small compartment above our seats. She thanked me with a thick Spanish accent and sat beside me. Minutes later, she handed me a folded piece of paper with a typed note on it.

The note informed me of her name and that she could not speak English. She was traveling back to her home country of Bogotá and had severe tendonitis in her hands. The note closed with a plea for help with her baggage and a kind word of thanks. I smiled at her and tried to explain that our connecting flights in Toronto would be in the same general location. I told her I would do my best to help her out.

Well, our flight ended up being very late leaving Calgary. For some reason, the authorities felt it unsafe to travel at 35 000 feet with a tiny glitch in our air system. I glanced down at my watch as we finally became airborne and realized this was going to cause a very tight window for me to connect to my Trinidad flight. It would, however, be an even tighter one for my Bogotá-bound companion.

Starting to get a little anxious about the timing of events, I tracked down an attendant and explained the situation. She spoke Spanish and arranged for the lady to get up into the front of the line while I stayed with the herd of cattle in the back of the plane. I was thankful she would get a good head start, but my heart was racing as I began to ponder my own particular situation. As the passengers at the front began to disembark, I knew my plight was really no better than my traveling companion's.

Trying to smile and apologizing the whole time, I politely started shoving my way through the crowd in the rear of the plane. I communicated my connection woes as justification for my seeming rudeness. I got out of the plane and took off running. It wasn't long before I caught up with my fragile companion, left alone in the airport to fend for herself like a wounded deer. She was struggling to hold on to her baggage and to figure out where to go all at the same time.

My heart melted. I ran up to her and grabbed her bag, telling her to do her best to run with me. She tried, but I needed to stop a few times and wait for her. During one of those pauses, I heard the 'last call' for both my flight and hers. Knowing I was in for a three-day stay over in Toronto if I didn't make it on that flight didn't help matters. I debated the evolutionary instinct of 'every man for himself'. But I looked at her and knew she was helplessly in the same predicament, and I couldn't leave her.

We began running again. Fortunately, I spotted an angel behind the wheel of a golf cart. I flagged down the flashing orange lights and quickly explained the situation. We got my new friend and her luggage onto the cart and off we went to our respective gate numbers.

We arrived at her gate first. I got the bags she owned into her hands and pointed her in the right direction. She smiled and gently kissed my check. I got back on the cart, rushed to my gate, and boarded my plane with seconds to spare.

Once I caught my breath and calmed myself down a little, I began to think of that lady on the other plane. I could feel my eyes welling up with tears as I thought about our brief encounter.

Chances are that our paths will never cross again, but I believe our encounter wasn't by accident. I was able to be the hands and feet of Christ for a lady who was obviously out of her element and fearful. She was a gentle reminder to me that there is more to this existence than my own measly life and plans. She was able to remind me that missing my flight was not going to be the end of the world.

Of course, this is easy for me to say now in retrospect. But I believe the experience has taught me more than that. I am beginning to see the importance of sincerity in how I interact with my fellow man.

"Well," you say, "that is a nice little story." But I believe it's so much more. Who is to say that this encounter was not an example of our reasonable act of worship? Offering ourselves up to live a life of purity occurs when we are willing to let go of our own plans and allow God to work. Living out our lives as a reasonable act of worship means that we approach the situations life gives us with a sincere heart that tries to do the right thing. It means allowing ourselves the honour of playing second fiddle.

Jesus said that a piece of bread, a cup of water, or an article of clothing offered to our fellow man is an act done unto him (see Matthew 25:31-45). Approaching those around us with a sincere heart involves interaction with all pretences striped away. Saint Therese said that every menial thing we do should be offered up as an act of worship to God—it needs to be looked upon as our gift to him.

> **Offering ourselves up to live a life of purity occurs when we are willing to let go of our own plans and allow God to work.**

*To live of love, 'tis without stint to give,*
*And never count the cost, nor ask reward;*
*So, counting not the cost, I long to live*
*And show my dauntless love for Thee, dear Lord!*
~ Saint Therese of Lisieux[6]

Our worship is in the sincerity of the sacrifice—big or small. It is in the realization that our lives and our plans are really not as important as we like to think they are. Our sincerity allows us to live a life of purity before God with the absence of hypocrisy. This is offering ourselves up as a living sacrifice. This is our reasonable act of worship.

Easier said than done, I know. But we all need to start somewhere. Take today and live today—let tomorrow worry about itself. How can you show God your sincerity in everything that you have planned for today? How can you show others that same sincerity in your interactions with them? It may be as simple as asking someone how they are doing and listening to their answer.

> Our worship is in the sincerity of the sacrifice. It is in the realization that our lives and our plans are really not as important as we think they are.

# Chapter 4: Understanding Devotion

> For the grace of God has been revealed, bringing salvation to all people. And we are instructed to turn from godless living and sinful pleasures. We should live in this evil world with self-control, right conduct, and devotion to God.
>
> ~Titus 2:11–12

# Chapter 2

## Review of Literature

I just did a search on Google. The keyword? Devotion. The word got just shy of 36 million hits. It seems to be a popular topic in our world. After a quick examination of my choices, it looks like the top 100 have little to do with the word itself. Much of what came up was devotional readings for various religions, some meditative pictures, and even a couple of music bands and record labels.

But what does any of that really have to do with devotion? What does it mean to be devoted to something? Paul instructed Titus that we should live with devotion to God. What does that look like? How do we become devoted?

Peter was devoted to something. No, not the crazy fisherman Peter of the Bible, and not this crazy author Peter who is currently rambling on. This Peter was one of the main characters in the familiar C. S. Lewis classic, *The Lion, The Witch, and The Wardrobe*. He was an Englishman who found himself walking through a wardrobe and into an entirely mystical world. Many of you are familiar with this literary work and have now also seen the movie released by Walt Disney. Lewis's work is a wonderful allegory that uses the ruler of Narnia, Aslan the Lion, as a depiction of Jesus Christ.

**What does devotion look like? What does it mean to be devoted to something?**

Part 1: A Starting Ground

It is the battle scene that I want to draw your attention to. The day before, Aslan had met with the Witch to discuss the 'buying back' of Edmund's blood, and then spent a good portion of the day preparing Peter with instructions for battle...

> "...till at last Peter said, 'But you will be there yourself, Aslan.'
> 'I can give you no promise of that,' answered the Lion."[7]

On the morning of the battle, Aslan is gone, the girls are gone, and Peter is left with an army looking to him for leadership. Peter assumes his position in the absence of the Lion as the armies of the Witch draw near. In breath-taking scenery and with an emotional cry he raises high his sword. The sleek metal flashes against the sun as Peter issues the following decree:

"For Narnia...and for Aslan!"

Peter decides to put his life on the line for a country that is not his home and a Lion that is nowhere to be found. Why? Peter had discovered what true devotion was all about. Don't miss my point. Peter was not devoted to something because he knew everything there was to know. On the contrary, as far as he knew, he was fighting a loosing battle for a dead lion.

Peter didn't know that the Lion would rise and would conquer the Witch once and for all—he didn't know all that Aslan was accomplishing behind the scenes as Peter raised his sword to start the battle. However, he was willing to face death head-on for the object of his devotion...a Lion who wasn't safe, but was good.[8]

The reason? Peter's devotion came from relationship. Peter spent time with Aslan—he got to know this wild, untamed Lion in a way that would evoke both horror and envy in every creature of Narnia. Peter didn't have all the answers when he lifted up that sword—but he knew Aslan was worth fighting for because he had been in the presence of the Lion.

How about you? Have you been in the presence of the Lion? Have you spent time walking and talking with him? Have you allowed his eyes to pierce through your soul into the areas that no one else knows about? This is the beginning of true devotion.

> Have you been in the presence of the Lion? Have you spent time walking and talking with him? Have you allowed his eyes to pierce through your soul?

## YOUR ALABASTER JAR...

We are all devoted to something. There is an innate part of us that must give itself to worship. Some give themselves to sports, others to their work, others to family. Some of us even give ourselves to worthy causes and ministries. Many of us end up filling the devotion-sized hole in our life with material things instead of giving ourselves wholly to the true object of devotion.

There comes a time when each of us has to look at where our devotion truly lies. Mary did. Unlike her sister Martha, who was busy serving their guests, she was content to sit at the feet of Jesus and spend time with him. Even when Martha complained that she was doing all the work by herself, Jesus said Mary had the better idea (see Luke 10:38-42).

Let's now look in on another evening, just before Jesus begins his last stint in Jerusalem. It is a beautiful night on the sloping hills of Bethany. The stars are twinkling; the air is crisp. Jesus and his disciples are all over at Simeon's house for an evening get-together.[9] Also in attendance are Martha, Mary, and Lazarus—the three siblings so close to Jesus. Martha is busy getting the meal ready while Mary hangs out with the boys to hear the words of Jesus. No doubt, Jesus himself is reclining at the table with Lazarus and Simeon, discussing the events of the day. Some of the disciples are at the table as well; others are just outside breathing in the coolness of the night air.

> There comes a time when each of us has to look at where our devotion truly lies.

Then something happens. Something stirs in Mary. She gets up from the seating area and leaves for a moment. Martha is hopeful that she's coming in to help with the hors d'oeuvres, but that isn't the direction Mary heads. When she reappears, Mary has cupped in her hands the alabaster jar that she had been waiting for the just the right moment to use.

It was a beautiful jar made of finely-grained gypsum, so polished you could see through its delicate walls into the liquid resting inside. It was probably sealed at the top with some sort of wax so that the exquisite scent and the expensive substance would not escape. The substance contained within this treasured vessel was the essence of nard—an ointment carefully extracted from a perennial herb that only grew in the Himalayan Mountains.

Now was the moment. Mary had twelve ounces of this perfume inside the walls of the beautifully sealed container. This cup-and-a-half of fragrance held within the alabaster jar was worth an entire year's wages.

Can you picture it? Martha stops getting the meal ready. Lazarus sits up from his reclined position at the table and is watching intently, as are the others around him. The family dog has stopped chomping on its lamb chop and lies on the floor with paws out and ears perked. The disciples outside feel the hush inside and turn to look through the doorway and window. Everyone within earshot now has their head turned and their eyes fixed on Mary.

Mary doesn't see them. There is only one set of eyes into which she is gazing—the eyes of her Master. The carpenter's eyes peer back at her filled with love, compassion, and a hint of sadness at the prophetic meaning behind what is about to happen.

Mary kneels down and breaks the seal of her beautiful jar. The sound of the fracturing cap resonates throughout the entire room as the beautiful fragrance immediately spills into the air, reaching the nostrils of everyone around the pair. Mary slowly stands up, her eyes filling with emotion, and begins to pour the ointment over the head of her Lord. She continues, pouring more over his feet and washing them with her own hair. Everyone around is stunned. Some are even indignant. What could all of this mean?

> Mary doesn't see anything else. There is only one set of eyes into which she is gazing.

I believe what we have just witnessed was more than a true act of devotion. Yes, Mary showed great compassion for and devotion to her Saviour, but I think there is more to be said of her sacrifice. No doubt, that jar and its contents were very precious to her. You don't invest a year of your life into something and not pay special attention to it.

This jar could have been an object of Mary's devotion. However, in order to show her true devotion to Jesus, she let go of something that was dear and costly to her, breaking the seal of one devotion for the love of the other. Yes, she was preparing the body of her Saviour for burial, but I believe she was also allowing a part of her own soul to die—a part that she realized didn't matter in light of the one who was sitting in front of her.

We all have objects of devotion. We all have stuff in our lives vying for the one seat available in our hearts. Perhaps we say that God is our one devotion, but do our deeds match our words? Do the thoughts of our hearts line up with the actions of our tongues, the actions of our bodies? We need to take some time to painfully consider this. What are the objects of our devotion?

What's in your alabaster jar? What talent or resource is God tugging on your heart about? Maybe it's your finances, maybe it is a relationship. Perhaps it's time to break the seal. Perhaps it's time to pour out that one object of devotion trying to hold itself above the true object of your devotion. Maybe it's time, with tears in your eyes, to fall at his feet and declare to him once and for all that you are willing to be poured out as an offering to him—that you are willing to live your life in purity. Declare to him that you are prepared, against everything else, to offer yourself to him as a reasonable act of worship.

> We all have objects of devotion. We all have stuff vying for the one seat available in our hearts. What's in your alabaster jar?

## FROM INNER DEVOTION COMES INNER CHANGE...

Mary had inner devotion to her Lord. Peter had inner devotion to Aslan. I believe this inner devotion is the key to unlocking change within our lives. This is the change required for us to walk through this process of purity on two feet instead of stumbling around on all fours.

Why is inner devotion the key? Because inner change is going to hurt. That's why so many of us don't bother trying anymore—we don't want to deal with the stuff that inner change requires us to deal with. Dr Larry Crabb describes the feeling this way:

> If awareness of what's inside forces me to admit that I'm utterly dependent on resources outside my control for the kind of change I desire, if helplessness really is at the core of my existence, I prefer to live on the surface of things. It's far more comfortable. To admit I cannot deal with all that's within me strikes a deathblow to my claim to self-sufficiency. To deny the

frightening realities within my soul seems as necessary to life as breathing.[10]

Truly walking the process of purity involves digging deeper than a superficial relationship with our God. It forces us to deal with some key things along the way that cause us some pain, some hurt, and some frustration. So many times, we back away when Christ comes close because we don't want to go through the pain that change requires.

> Inner devotion is the key because inner change is going to hurt.

It's not enough to set a standard and then rely on sheer willpower to see that standard through. It's not enough to tell yourself that you will never neglect your children again or that you will never put work over your relationship with Christ. I am sure you are as painfully aware of this fact as I am. Instead, we need to begin to search our hearts for the reasons behind our actions—we need to be willing to be ploughed up. C. S. Lewis observes in *Mere Christianity*:

> It is like that here. The terrible thing, the almost impossible thing, is to hand over your whole self—all your wishes and precautions—to Christ. But it is far easier than what we are all trying to do instead. For what we are trying to do is to remain what we call 'ourselves', to keep personal happiness as our great aim in life, and yet at the same time be 'good'. We are all trying to let our mind and heart go their own way—centered on money or pleasure or ambition—and hoping, in spite of this, to behave honestly and chastely and humbly. And that is exactly what Christ warned us you could not do. As He said, a thistle cannot produce figs. If I am a field that contains nothing but grass-seed, I cannot produce wheat. Cutting the grass may keep it short: but I shall still produce grass and no wheat. If I want to produce wheat, the change must go deeper than the surface. I must be ploughed up and re-sown.
>
> ~ C. S. Lewis[11]

That's where devotion comes in. Inner devotion unlocks the door to inner change instead of us bumbling around trying to break the wall down in our own strength and pride. If we know, truly know, who we are fighting for, we will be willing to struggle through the pain of change. Holy Spirit is there to help, and we know that at the end of the day it will be worth it. Inner change is not able to happen without inner devotion. And inner devotion will not take place unless time is spent with your Lion.

> If we know, truly know, who we are fighting for, we will be willing to struggle through the pain of change.

So, we have walked ourselves back to the beginning of this chapter. How is your relationship with Christ? Whether you have had a relationship with him for five minutes or fifty years, how is it going? How deep have you allowed your devotion to him to run? What are you willing to let go of in order to get closer to him?

There was a period of my life during my first few years at university when I reached a real low point. I was struggling with some key habits in my life and it seemed like I was going nowhere. On the outside, I remained the 'have it all together' worship leader and son of prominent people within my church. On the inside, though, I was depressed and my soul was in anguish. A close friend and mentor suggested that I go see a counsellor—a third party I could talk to without feeling that need to have it all together.

For about six months, I spent an hour with this counsellor every two weeks. No one knew but this one friend. I had the advantage of commuting by myself to college at the time, so I always seemed to have a 'late lab' one night, which gave me some space in my schedule.

It was an interesting few months. In some respects, I felt worse than before I started the sessions, and I continued to feel like a complete hypocrite. I felt the need to perform, and I was scared to let anyone see the real me—the me that was broken and confused. I believed that if I allowed people in, they would see me only as some sinner beyond God's grace.

I went to this counsellor to get fixed. I had problems with sin in my life and I wanted to know how to rectify those problems. I wanted to know the steps to freedom. I wanted to follow a set formula of incantations and offerings—a quick fix so I could move on in my 'together' fashion.

Do you know what my counsellor said? He said I was looking too much at the sin I was trying to get rid of and not enough at my relationship with the Sinless One. He encouraged me to take my eyes off of myself and concentrate instead on my relationship with and devotion to Christ. In essence, I believe he was trying to tell me to not get so caught up in my pursuit of living a pure and holy life that I neglected my devotion to the Pure and Holy One.

I pulled out of the counselling after a few months, partly because I didn't feel we were going anywhere. Maybe it was because I wasn't ready to hear what he had to say. Maybe I wasn't ready to allow the walls to come down and to be real and vulnerable with someone. Several years later, I look back on that time of my life and am beginning to realize the importance of his message.

> **We need to be careful not to get so caught up in our pursuit of living a pure and holy life that we neglect our devotion to the Pure and Holy One.**

This inner devotion God longs for us to have with him is a key to the personal transformation we long to experience within. Change will not come within our lives unless we understand who it is we are changing for. If we are trying to change because we want people to see us as someone who 'has it all together', we are going to fail miserably. It needs to go deeper than that. Like Peter, we will not be able to raise our sword and face our death unless we believe in why we are doing it. Like Mary, we need to be willing to see that the treasures we may have are worth nothing compared to the time we spend in the presence of our Saviour.

We are about to journey into the second part of this book together. It's going to get into the nitty gritty—the 'what does living a pure life look like?' sort of thing. But I don't believe we are able to look correctly at some of these steps if our heart is not where it should be. That's why we have focused here first.

> If the devotion is not within us, the ability to change will not be either. Change will not come within our lives unless we understand who it is we are changing for.

I think it's time you went for another walk. Perhaps I should too. Ask yourself some of the key questions we have looked at. What areas of purity are the hardest for you? What are you looking at when you glance at the person in the mirror? Are you approaching your God and the people around you sincerely, or do you only have your own interests in mind? Who or what is the true object of your devotion?

Please don't rush this. The practical and formulaic part of life is helpful to us only if we have laid the correct foundation. Rome wasn't built in a day, and succeeding in this life of faith is not an overnight deal. Spend some time away from here and get to know your creator a little better. I'll be right here when you're ready to read on.

I'll catch you on the other side of that walk.

# Part 2: A Battleground

O Sovereign LORD, my strong savior, you protected me on the day of battle.

~Psalm 140:7

For we are not fighting against people made of flesh and blood, but against the evil rulers and authorities of the unseen world, against those mighty powers of darkness who rule this world, and against wicked spirits in the heavenly realms.

~Ephesians 6:12

# Chapter 5:
# A Confusing Situation

Oh, what a miserable person I am! Who will free me from this life that is dominated by sin? Thank God! The answer is in Jesus Christ, our Lord.

~Romans 7:24-25a

Sometimes I just don't get it. We see it on the news. We see it in our neighbourhood and throughout our country. We watch the people around us and end up just giving our heads a shake from time to time. What were they thinking? Why would they do that? We live in a world where people have one-night-stands in the name of love and twice-a-year church in the name of religion. We live in a world where many celebrities pour their hearts and wallets into saving panda bears and seals while not lifting a finger to help starving children in countries infested with drought and disease. We live in a world where people kill in the name of life and superficially blame horrible epidemics like AIDS on living immoral lifestyles.

We live in a world of chaos.

Perhaps, though, the chaos we see in the world outside of us is really only reflective of the chaos that is inside each one of us. For as long as we have the capacity to allow oxygen into our lungs, we will face a confusing world called life. We struggle with thought patterns and actions. Digging deeper than thoughts, we toil with a longing for something that is greater

> **Perhaps the chaos we see in the world outside of us is really only reflective of the chaos that is inside each one of us.**

## Part 2: A Battleground

than what we are experiencing on this earth. And you know what? We were created that way. We were never created to be fully content with life on this earth.

> Beneath the surface of everyone's life, especially the more mature, is an ache that will not go away. It can be ignored, disguised, mislabeled, or submerged by a torrent of activity, but it will not disappear. And for good reason. We were designed to enjoy a better world than this. And until that better world comes along, we will groan for what we do not have. *An aching soul is evidence not of neurosis or spiritual immaturity, but of realism.*
>
> ~ Larry Crabb[12]

As of yet, that better world hasn't come along. So, while we stand in this one's current core, we each have battles to face. In the middle of facing our own deep longings for things yet to come, we are also confronted with the fact that the world we live in has been inundated with sin since shortly after the dawn of time.

We all have some key problems when it comes to living our lives with purity. It may not look the same for you as it does for me, but there are common underlying issues. These are the issues we need to deal with.

**We all have something. What it is really doesn't matter. The sin is just an outward manifestation of an inward struggle.**

We all have something. We all have a struggle, a temptation, a habit. No doubt, we all have more than one. Perhaps for you, it's gaining control of your temper. Maybe it's keeping the door of the fridge closed. Maybe it's keeping your hands out of someone else's (or your own) pants. Maybe it's admitting that you don't have all the answers. What it is really doesn't matter to me because the sin is just the outward manifestation of the inward struggle. When we look inside, each of us faces the same battle—the battle to walk through the process of living a pure life in the midst of a confusing world.

## THE GOSPEL ACCORDING TO SAINT PAUL...

The world was just as confusing and the battle was just as strong for a man named Paul. The Apostle Paul was a man who knew both sides of the coin when it came to the early Christian church. He grew up well trained in the Torah and well versed in pharisaical law.

> *For I was circumcised when I was eight days old, having been born into a pure-blooded Jewish family that is a branch of the tribe of Benjamin. So I am a real Jew if there ever was one! What's more, I was a member of the Pharisees, who demand the strictest obedience to the Jewish law.*
>
> *~ Philippians 3:5*

His own credentials proved he was a good Jew—one that God got a hold of and changed forever. Paul had an encounter with the risen Christ and went on to be, in many respects, the founding father of the Gentile Christian church as well as the most prolific author of the New Testament. Paul was the first Christian theologian, and yet he struggled with many of the same things you and I do today.

Take your time and read through Romans 7:14–25, and you will get a good glimpse of the struggle. Let me share with you some snippets...

> I don't understand myself at all (v. 15)
>
> I really want to do what is right, but I don't do it (v. 15)
>
> I do the very thing I hate (v. 15)

> I know perfectly well that what I am doing is wrong (v. 16)
> I can't help myself (v. 17)
> I am rotten through and through (v. 18)
> When I try not to do wrong, I do it anyway (v. 19)
> It seems to be a fact of life (v. 21)

I don't think it an overstatement that many would consider Paul to be one of the greatest Christian leaders history has left us with. Knowing this, I can't help but admire his honesty—I can't help but envy his vulnerability. He was ready to put himself out there. He was willing to let people see the struggles he faced so that we might all work through some of this together. I wonder what our Christian world would be like today if our leaders were willing to do the same.

> **Who can help but admire Paul's honesty? Who can help but envy his vulnerability? What would the Christian world be like today if our leaders were willing to follow his example?**

It's sort of comforting to know that Paul struggled with the same things I do. In fact, the Christian church as a whole has continued in this struggle with sin ever since Paul wrote his letter. In the mid 1700s, Robert Robinson co-wrote a famous hymn that many churches still sing today. "Come Thou Fount of Every Blessing" has inspired countless Christians in mainstream and traditional churches alike. Take a read through verse 3 with me...

> *O to grace how great a debtor*
> *Daily I'm constrained to be!*
> *Let Thy goodness like a fetter*
> *Bind my wandering heart to Thee*
> *Prone to wander, Lord, I feel it*
> *Prone to leave the God I love;*

> *Here's my heart, O take and seal it,*
> *Seal it for Thy courts above.*[13]

In essence, Robinson was saying, "God, if left by myself, I will not be good, so please don't leave me." Some two thousand years have passed since Paul was on the earth, and almost 250 years since Robinson bore his soul. We still find ourselves with the same struggles. In a nutshell, we have been given a sinful nature as a result of Adam and Eve's fall that has tried to jockey for position in our life since we came out of the womb.

But there is hope, even while we remain on this earth. Christ's death on the cross has cancelled sin's stronghold in our life once and for all. Jesus Christ became the ultimate sacrifice for the sins of the entire world so that we might be free from the grip of our old nature.

> *Sin is no longer your master, for you are no longer subject to the law, which enslaves you to sin. Instead you are free by God's grace.*
> ~ *Romans 6:14*

I want you to notice that the verse you just read is from Romans chapter six. It's not until the next chapter that Paul begins to share his own personal battles. Paul declares that we are no longer subject to the Law and that we are freed by God's grace *before* he shares his own inner struggle to live out that freedom. Paul's letter on its first read can seem rather confusing. But I think one of the messages Paul conveys to his readers is the importance of the process. Paul knew there would still be a battle to fight. This is the process of living our lives as a reasonable act of worship. This lifelong battle is really what worship is all about.

If you have asked Jesus to be Lord of your life, then sin no longer has a grip on you. Yet while you live on this earth, you will struggle with sin as it tries to regain control over you. Some days you are victorious, some days you are not. Sometimes the 'some days' that you are not victorious begin to add up and allow an inner purity issue to tighten its grip on your life. Does this mean you have lost your salvation? Not necessarily. But it does mean you might have some tough work ahead of you. With the help of Holy Spirit, and a willingness on our part, we can get to that inner change required to properly live out our lives as an offering of worship.

> One of the messages Paul conveys to his readers is the importance of the process. This lifelong battle is really what worship is all about.

In order to live out this process, we need to have an understanding of...

1. Where we have come from.
    - Because we are descendants of Adam, we have been born with a sinful nature (Romans 5:12).
    - None of us, on our own, have the ability to reach the standard of holiness that God has set in place (Romans 3:23).

2. What Christ has done.
    - Christ Jesus died that we might be freed from our sins (Romans 3:25).
    - Through Christ we are no longer condemned (Romans 8:1).
    - We are no longer controlled by our sinful nature but by the Spirit of God living within us (Romans 8:9).

3. Where we are to go from here.
    - We are called to continually live out God's work in our lives (Philippians 2:12).

- God has promised to be faithful to help us (Philippians 1:6).
- We need to ask Holy Spirit for the power to change (Romans 7:6).

Volumes of books have been written on this subject, and I am not so naïve as to think that my synopsis of Paul's theology has shown you every angle. That's not the purpose of this book. We want to look at how to live out this process, but I think it's important to know why it can be a little confusing at times.

So take heart. You're not alone. Yes, God has paid the penalty for sin once and for all. Yes, you are no longer under the Law or bound to the Law. Yes, the things you struggle with have been the same temptations and issues since the beginning of time. But you are not called to give up and give in just because what ails you has been common to mankind forever. You still have a battle to face and a part to play in this thing, so let's continue our journey together.

## A HEALTHY DOSE OF FEAR AND GRACE...

I think there are a few other things we need to understand in the midst of the confusion between what has been done for us and what is left for us to do. I think we need to have a clear comprehension of the balance between revering the absolute holiness of God and accepting the unimaginable and unconditional love of that same God. In other words, it's important that we have healthy doses of both fear and grace. If we don't, the result is never good.

Perhaps Ananias and Sapphira are two of the best New Testament examples of people who did not quite understand the result of messing around with a holy God. Holy Spirit had descended upon the people of the early church, enabling them to perform many miraculous signs and wonders. The congregants of the church banded together, selling property and valuables to help those in need.

> We need to have a clear comprehension of the balance between revering the absolute holiness of God and accepting the unimaginable and unconditional love of that same God.

This husband and wife team decided to do the same, except they kept some of the money they made from their acreage for themselves.[14] Not a huge deal—it was theirs to do with as they pleased. It's not like the apostles were establishing a strictly communal society. But the rubber met the road when they *declared* they were giving *all* the money. Maybe they didn't want to look cheap. By most standards, we could chalk it up to a little white lie.

Unfortunately for this deceitful duo, that's not exactly how God looked at the ordeal. Peter declared that satan had filled Ananias's heart and the man instantly fell to the ground dead. His wife, not knowing what had occurred, came in shortly after and suffered the same consequence.

The result? "Great fear gripped the entire church and all others who heard what had happened" (Acts 5:11). Gee, ya think? I dare say, though, that it was a healthy dose of fear. God is not a vending machine. You can't use a token payment of respect in order to get some blessing from his hand. Our Christian evangelical society cries out for the manifested presence of God. I wonder how many of us would be dead on the ground if God granted our request. We need to be careful how we approach the presence of a holy God.

But there is the other side of this coin as well. Sometimes we completely forget that we serve a God of compassion, who is "slow to get angry, full of unfailing love and truth" (Psalm 86:15b). Paul said that where sin abounds, grace abounds all the more (Romans 5:20, NKJV).

Joseph's brothers did not have an understanding of grace. These ten siblings kidnapped Joseph the dreamer, threw him into a pit, and then sold him into slavery. They were jealous of their father's favour. Some twenty years later, Joseph was second-in-command of Egypt and his brothers came begging for food. The brothers don't recognize him, but the colourful coat owner knew them, and he tested them to see if their hearts had changed. After three nights in jail the brothers could only blame themselves:

> God is not a vending machine. We cannot use a token payment of respect in order to get some blessing from his hand. We need to be careful how we approach the presence of a holy God.

> *Speaking among themselves, they said, "This has all happened because of what we did to Joseph long ago. We saw his terror and anguish and heard his pleadings, but we wouldn't listen. That's why this trouble has come upon us."*
> ~ *Genesis 42:21*

The brothers had no idea of the bigger picture. They just assumed that the sins they committed so long ago were now coming back to haunt them. The brothers didn't understand how God could take a wrong they had done and weave it into his plan for good. The God they knew was harsh and unyielding. They had no conception of grace, but they were about to get a large dose of it. They were about to find out that they served not only a God of holiness and justice, but also a God of grace.

I think a lot of times the church decides to camp out in one of these two lines of thought. Some of us preach fire and brimstone to the point that Christians live in complete fear of stepping out of line and slipping down into the pit of hell, causing them not to have any real relationships with God or man. Others preach God's love and forgiveness to the extent that people come to terms with accepting immoral lifestyles because 'God loves us anyway and we are not bound to the Law.' Both directions are extremely dangerous, and the conflict between them is probably the reason why so many societies look upon Christianity as a hypocritical institution that has lost any real effectiveness in a messed up world.

> We seem to camp out in one of these two lines of thought, causing a society on the outside to view the church only as a hypocritical institution.

In order to live out a life of purity, we need to be careful that we don't let the pendulum swing too far in either direction. We need to keep a healthy dose of both fear and grace to walk the path Christ has laid out before us.

## BE WILLING TO GO DEEPER THAN THE SKIN...

I live in suburbia. Really, the city is laid out so that I don't have to go more than ten minutes to get everything I need. I am in a self-contained little community, close to the edge of the city limits. As I drive around, though, billboards try their best to convince me that shopping downtown is really where it's at. Their slogan...

"Who you are starts at the core"

As I drove past one of these signs this afternoon it dawned on me—that's true! Who I am starts in the core of my being. It's not enough for me to superficially live my life on the outside if the core of my being is hurting. It's not enough to follow pharisaical rules that make me look like I have it all together if the very centre of my being is full of malice, impure thoughts, or greed.

Dr. Larry Crabb is a Christian psychologist, author, and professor. In his book, *Inside Out*, he deals with this issue of forcing ourselves to go beyond the superficiality of skin-deep Christianity and to compel ourselves to take a closer and deeper look.

> Outside cleanliness, whether the product of zeal or of complacency does not impress our Lord. With relentless penetration, He intends to deal with the filth we try to keep hidden beneath the surface. To live life as God intends requires that we uncover the dirt and learn what we must do to participate in the cleaning process. We must take an inside look.[15]

You see, the inner change that we talked about in chapter four cannot occur unless we are willing to take that inner look. In the midst of the confusion between being saved and living out our salvation, between living a life marked by grace and a life marked by fear, we need to be willing to dig deep and examine our hearts. What are the motives behind our actions? Why are we living the way we are? Whether good or bad, we need to take the time to examine ourselves—to look inside so that we might begin to change.

God is not looking for people who have it all together. He is looking for people who are willing to accept the price he has paid and to work on living out their lives in the light of this paid transaction. He is looking for people who are willing to face

> God is looking for people who are willing to accept the price he has paid and to work on living out their lives in the light of this paid transaction.

their hurts, their disappointments, and their sins while allowing him to reshape, to remould, and to rebuild them into his very own image. Are you willing to be that person? It's a lifetime of work, and it won't be fully complete until you see him face to face. But he promises, if you'll let him, to be with you every step of the way (Philippians 1:6). We have reason to be encouraged in our journey!

    Who we are really does start at the core. Thankfully, the God we serve is willing to start there as well. Are you?

# Chapter 6: Living Sacrifice

And so, dear brothers and sisters, I plead with you to give your bodies to God. Let them be a living and holy sacrifice—the kind he will accept. When you think of what he has done for you, is this too much to ask?

~Romans 12:1

And now, God is building you, as living stones, into his spiritual temple. What's more, you are God's holy priests, who offer the spiritual sacrifices that please him because of Jesus Christ.

~1 Peter 2:5

Sacrifice. In many respects, we have completely lost the meaning of this word within our wealthy western world. We don't really understand the concept of giving something up because we often have no need to give it up. We have money to buy the things we need, and credit to buy the things we want. We have fast food restaurants and drive-through bank machines so that we don't need to sacrifice our time. We have blackberries and palm pilots, computers and cell phones that allow us to be everywhere at all times and nowhere at any one time.

Yet we say we make *sacrifices*—the word comes up in numerous discussions, debates, and decisions. The husband who gives up his Friday evening to go to the opera with his wife instead of the football game with the boys. Is this true sacrifice? The wife who forfeits a lucrative career in the business world and chooses instead to raise a family and build a home. Is this true sacrifice? What about the teenage girl who gives in to her boyfriend's request in hopes of obtaining his undying love. Is this true sacrifice?

The three scenarios I have mentioned are obviously all very different. Some are noble, others are not. But the word sacrifice can be (and has been) used in each one of them. So what does the word sacrifice mean when it comes to our spiritual walk? Why would Paul urge us to let our bodies be living sacrifices? Why would Peter talk of our priestly role involving the offering of spiritual sacrifices? What does this offering look like in the humdrum of our daily walk?

A quick look in the dictionary will give you a phrase like 'offering up'. Whenever we are sacrificing something, we are giving that which we have control over to another object, person, or deity. In other words, if we are offering something up, we are, in essence, letting it go. I think this is a key to our whole discussion on becoming living sacrifices.

> **If we are offering something up, we are in essence letting it go. This is a key to becoming living sacrifices.**

> You will never know what God has in store for you unless you are willing to let go of whatever holds you where you don't really want to be.

Perhaps that is why so many of us seem stuck—the word sacrifice involves letting go. For some reason, we have a hard time letting go. Perhaps it is that we don't trust God to provide if we do let go. Perhaps we are too comfortable taking care of things our own way.

Perhaps it is time to shift our thinking.

The story has been told of a little girl who sees a string of fake pearls in a dollar store. She saves up her allowance so she can buy these pearls, and cherishes them like they were worth millions of dollars. They are around her neck whenever possible, and she loves the way they shine against her fair skin.

One day, as her father tucks the little girl into bed, he asks if he can have her pearls. The little girl greatly loves her father and becomes distraught, offering him anything else but her beautiful pearls. The father smiles, says that's okay, and tucks the covers close around her, kissing her good night as he steps out the door.

Each night, the scenario continues. The father asks his little girl for the pearls and the little girl offers anything but. The father simply smiles and tucks her in for the night. One night, the father enters the room to see his little girl on the bed, crying. He asks her what's wrong. She says nothing, but looks up into his loving eyes and offers him the pearls she so deeply cherishes.

The father smiles, takes the pearls, and pulls out of his pocket a beautiful box. Inside, the little girl finds a set of real pearls. The father has had them all along, just waiting for the little girl to give up what she held on to so dearly.[16]

I think there's something in each one of us that our loving Father is asking us to release. We all have dollar store junk in our lives that God is asking us to surrender. Some of our junk might be comfortable sins or familiar habits that we have grown accustomed to. Some of our junk might also be good things—past successes or current ministries. Either way, for reasons we don't always see, our Father is asking us to let go of them.

> **We all have dollar store junk in our lives that God is asking us to surrender. We need to trust in our Father.**

Letting go can be a hard thing. Sacrifice is not easy. But we need to trust our Father; he will never ask us to let go of something if it isn't in our best interest.

## MOUNTING YOUR ALTAR...

One young man, one old man. The two walk side by side. Neither says much, for they do not need to—their relationship has a closeness that goes beyond mere words. It is a father and his son ...a senior man of faith and a junior man of vision. The two have been on their arduous hike for three long days, and both father and son are beginning to feel tired under the hot, dry heat of the Palestinian sun.

It is the last day of their journey. The duo begins in the cool of the morning, before the sun brings its heat to the land. Although the morning air is quiet and comfortable, there is a certain heaviness in the atmosphere around them. These mountainous regions were known for sudden shifts in the weather, but this heaviness did not come from outside. Rather, it was the weight felt by an inner storm—an inner turmoil that was raging within the father.

The son felt it as well, but did not know why. Confusion troubled his heart, and he could not bring himself to a state of peace. He had been on these sacrificial trips with his father many times, but this time was different. Something was wrong, and he couldn't figure out what it was. His father became ever quieter as they hiked along, side by side, watching the beautiful sun as it slowly began to peek across the desert horizon and rise into the eastern sky.

The father glanced over at the son he was so proud of—his promised miracle that God had given after so many years. There were times during his wife's long barren years when he must have doubted that God could come through. His human nature had to have struggled with the possibility that his wife could become pregnant when she was nearing the century mark. Now the very flesh of his flesh was a constant reminder of the faithfulness of Yahweh. His eyes filled up with tears as he remembered taking many of these same walks with his son. They had rejoiced together and he had taught his son all of the ways of Jehovah.

How was he going to explain this to his son, his treasure? How was God going to fulfill his promise if this really was the requirement? What was he going to tell his wife and family back home? What was he going to do? The questions obliterated any space left in his mind. Maybe he hadn't heard right—God could not possibly want this...could he? The man and the boy continued to walk, and the silent turmoil was carried with them as the heat of the day began to set over the land.

Can you feel the tension? Can you feel the inward struggle that this father and son team faced? I am sure Abraham felt it as he led his son up the mountain and prepared to give God the one thing he treasured more than his own life.

Abraham was a man of faith, and it was his belief in God's promise that was credited to him as righteousness (Genesis 15:6). This man made the famous 'hall of faith' described in Hebrews 11 and is looked upon in both the Christian and Jewish communities as a strong pillar of faith. And rightly so. But Abraham was not without human flesh. Hebrews 11:19 states that Abraham believed that even if he had to slay Isaac, God would resurrect him. But the human side of him must have questioned God's plan from time to time. I believe there had to have been moments during the journey when doubt tried to worm its way into the mind of this confident man.

Read the story in Genesis 22 and put yourself there—feel the heat of the sun and the heaviness in the air. Allow yourself to experience what both Abraham and Isaac must have been feeling as Isaac poses the question of where the lamb for the sacrifice will come from (v. 7).

Now that we have the picture painted, let's dig a little deeper—let's go underneath the surface. We know that the altars used in Biblical days to sacrifice animals before God were often over four feet off the ground.[17] We also know that, by this time, Abraham was a very old man—well past the century mark. The old man's strength could not have been what it once was in his youthful days. Isaac, on the other hand, was in the prime of his life, a young boy close to twenty with strength to spare.

Keep this picture fresh in your mind, because knowing this changes the scenery (and perhaps the message) of our story a little. I remember growing up with my picture Bible and seeing the picture of Abraham tying his son's hands behind his back. Today, however, I want to suggest a slightly different view...

Part 2: A Battleground

> There is no way Abraham could have tied his son up
> and placed him on top of that altar
> unless Isaac willingly surrendered.

Ouch. There's the punch line. Isaac had to have mounted his own altar. He willingly laid down his life in order to please his father. He had all the visions a young boy could ever have, and I believe that, had he wanted to, he could have defended and freed himself easily. Yet he willingly mounted the altar and prepared to give up his life. As a result, Isaac became the next integral part of the blessing and special plan that God had for the children of Israel.

Both men were tested that day. Abraham was tested to give up what he loved, and Isaac was tested to lay down his life and mount his own altar. Both men passed the test, and a lamb provided the replacement for the sacrifice that God still required, a foreshadowing of the spotless Lamb taking our place and making the ultimate sacrifice for the sins of mankind.

There are altars in each of our lives that our Heavenly Father is asking us to mount... altars to place our pride on, altars to leave our sin at. There are places to sacrifice our selfish desires and impure motives. God has given us free choice and free will. He will not force us to get up on those altars. He would rather that the choice be left in our hands. Are we willing to submit to his plan for our lives, or will we choose one that is self-created?

> There are altars in each of
> our lives that we are being
> asked to mount.
> Are we willing to submit to
> his plan for our lives,
> or will we choose one that is
> self-created?

Isaac chose his father's plan and reaped the blessings thereof. Likewise, we can reap the blessings of our Father's plan or the consequences of the one we choose instead. The blessings that come from mounting our altars tend not to be readily seen in this earthly realm. God requires that we allow ourselves to be sacrificed—that we allow our nature to die. There's no replacement in this sacrifice—each of us is required to lay down and let go of our own ambitions and desires for the sake of a greater call.

What altar is God asking you to mount today? Perhaps it is that one small thing you have been entertaining in your mind that causes your life to reside with a residue of impurity (see Ephesians 5:3). Perhaps it is the ministry that you have poured your heart and soul into. Perhaps it is a relationship with someone or the comfortable position you currently find yourself in. Ministries and healthy relationships are not bad in and of themselves, but sometimes God may ask us to lay them down and concentrate on him alone.

Paul encouraged us in Romans 12:1 to offer our bodies as living sacrifices, which is our true spiritual act of worship. Have you presented your body to God? Have you mounted the altar and laid all your desires and hopes before him? It is not something that we can accomplish in our own strength—we need to ask Holy Spirit to empower us in the process.

> Do you know what the problem is with *living* sacrifices? We keep crawling off the altar! If we were dead, we would just lie there. But in our human weakness, we fluctuate between truly wanting to entrust ourselves completely to God and taking back our lives to manage them on our own. When we try to do things in our own strength, we usually fall flat. Then our loving Father has to pick us up and put us back on the altar so that we can, by his mercies, be the living sacrifices he has called us to be.
>
> ~ Kimberly Hahn[18]

Have you sacrificed your dreams and comforts for him? Have you laid your fears and your concerns on the altar? The act of sacrifice is never a pleasant thing, but the rewards of becoming closer to our Heavenly Father and following his ultimate plan for our lives are far worth the cost. That decision, however, has been left up to you. Your extended hand will be the open door for God to pick you up and help you onto the altar.

> God is asking you to lay down some things.
> God is asking you to let go of some things.
> Will you mount your altar?

## WHEN DESIRE IS ABSENT FROM THE EQUATION...

Let's be honest, though. There are several times a day when the desire to extend my hand and have God get me back on that altar of living sacrifice just isn't there. Often my desire to give my spiritual and reasonable act of worship is lacking. I choose to get off the altar and don't *want* to get back on. My inward desire doesn't meet what I know my outward action needs to be. What do I do then?

Do it anyway. God doesn't call us to be controlled or led by our desires. That's probably one of the reasons the divorce rate among Christians is just as high as our secular counterparts. We don't know how to cope with life if we don't feel like coping. That's totally unbiblical, and we have to be very careful of living a life based on feelings alone.

C. S. Lewis wrote a collection of fictional letters from a head demon, Screwtape, to his nephew, Wormwood, a subordinate demon being trained in the masterful art of demonry. Lewis's masterpiece, *The Screwtape Letters*, gives us a great picture of our own lives and the stupidity we often allow. Let's look in on one of those letters for a moment.

To set the scene, Screwtape is writing to Wormwood concerning the young demon's assignment—an English soldier who has just come to faith in Jesus Christ. As you will read in the quote below, Screwtape warns his nephew of the potential danger of a Christian who is willing to obey despite their lack of desire.

> It is during such trough periods, much more than during the peak periods, that it [the newly converted soldier] is growing into the sort of creature He [God] wants it to be. Hence the prayers offered in the state of dryness are those which please Him best. We can drag our patients along by continual tempting, because we design them only for the table, and the more their will is interfered with the better. He cannot "tempt" to virtue as we do to vice. He wants them to learn to walk and must therefore take away His hand; and if only the will to walk is really there He is pleased even with their stumbles. Do not be deceived, Wormwood. Our cause is never more in danger than when a human, no longer desiring, but still intending, to do our Enemy's [God's] will, looks round upon a universe from which every trace of Him seems to have vanished, and asks why he has been forsaken, and still obeys.[19]

You see, desire is not always going to be there. One of the things God is desperate for us to learn is how to act on his will against our feelings or desires.

I think we often look at will and desire as the same thing. Our feelings lead us astray because of our fickle human nature. We have a fleshly desire to take our frustrations out on our family; we desire to take a second look at the girl in the office beside us; we desire to do all of these things that are outside of God's will.

> **God doesn't call us to be controlled or led by our desires. We have to be very careful of living a life based on feelings alone.**

Our will must conform to God's will, not to our desires. But instead, we allow our will to match our desires and end up stumbling. More often than not, living a pure life is the farthest thing from our natural desires.

> *The old sinful nature loves to do evil, which is just opposite from what the Holy Spirit wants. And the Spirit gives us desires that are opposite from what the sinful nature desires. These two forces are constantly fighting each other, and your choices are never free from this conflict.*
>
> ~ Galatians 5:17

It is within this constant conflict of choices that we are called to combat. We talk of breaking addictions in our lives and try to do so by sheer willpower. I would suggest that sheer willpower does not work. When our will is lined up with our natural desires, breaking addictive habits in our life seems impossible—the will of our human nature is stronger than we can fight against. We must invite Holy Spirit to help us line up our will with God's will. When this occurs, we will have the strength we need. Only then, in the midst of feeling like God is far from us and that his hand is no longer upon us, are we still able to obey simply because we know it's the right thing to do.

> **One of the things God is desperate for us to learn is how to act on his will against our feelings or desires.**

Some of you may be reading along wondering if this can ever be accomplished. The answer to your questioning mind is a resounding yes! Don't be discouraged in this battle. Sure, it would be nicer if our journey was more like a cakewalk than the climbing of Mount Everest, but you have the creator of the mountains as your guide. He knows every cavern and he'll be with you each step of the way. Sure, it can feel like the air is a little thin when you're trying to walk this high road of purity, but Holy Spirit is with you to supply everything you need for the journey.

## Chapter 6: Living Sacrifice

> *And God is able to make all grace abound to you, so that in all things at all times, having all that you need, you will abound in every good work.*
>
> ~ *2 Corinthians 9:8 (NIV)*

You have the best guide available to you for your journey. But the ultimate choice still gets left up to you. This is another 'rubber meets the road' moment—climbing up that altar and allowing yourself to be a living sacrifice when everything within you is crying out to go in some other direction. We need to press on. We need to continue even when the desire is not there. Screwtape understood the danger of the Spirit-led human committed to living through the process of purity even when his or her feelings don't match up. Later on, he gives further advice to his nephew to counteract this danger.

> **When our will is lined up with our natural desires, breaking addictive habits in our lives seem impossible. We must invite Holy Spirit to help.**

> In this...the thing to avoid is the total commitment. Whatever he *says*, let his inner resolution be not to bear whatever comes to him, but to bear it "for a reasonable period"—and let the reasonable period be shorter than the trial is likely to last. It need not be *much* shorter; in attacks on patience, chastity, and fortitude, the fun is to make the man yield just when (had he but known it) relief was almost in sight.[20]

How many times have we faced a battle of purity and given up because we saw no relief in sight? How many times have we lost that temper because we didn't see the other way out that was promised to us (see 1 Corinthians 10:13)? How many times have we turned to something else to fulfill our needs because we

Part 2: A Battleground

couldn't find God? How many times have we given up on God just seconds before the temptation would have been over?

We need to change our mindsets. We are in a battle and we cannot choose to fight only when we feel like it. We need to force ourselves upon that altar—to declare that we will do what we know is right even when we don't want to. We need to become the living sacrifices God has called each and every one of us to be.

> How many times have we given up on God just seconds before the temptation would have been over? We need to change our mindsets.

What is God calling you to let go of today? What 'pearls' are around your neck? What are you clutching so tightly that God is asking to be handed over to him? Are you willing to let go of what you want in exchange for what he wants? Are you willing to mount your altar? Are you willing to be the living sacrifice he is calling you to be?

# Chapter 7: Captive Thoughts

If you let them go with your troops into battle, you will be defeated no matter how well you fight.

~2 Chronicles 25:8a

We demolish arguments and every pretension that sets itself up against the knowledge of God, and we take captive every thought to make it obedient to Christ.

~2 Corinthians 10:5 (NIV)

I have never been behind bars. I have never heard the sound of the doors closing shut—the clash of metal against metal as bars intertwine with each other to secure the small 6' x 9' room called a cell. I can imagine it not being a very pleasant experience. To have the knowledge that you are now confined to this small space for a certain period of time must make even the toughest prisoner at least a little claustrophobic.

I have, however, been captive. I have been held against my will by the presence of love. I was six, she was seven, and she was heaven—a piece of ecstasy that had softly fallen down to earth with eyes so beautiful a boy could get lost in them for eternity. Soft flowing hair and a smile that directed your gaze to her fair complexion, her radiance, her beauty...

All right, I know, I was six at the time—perhaps it is a small exaggeration. But understand the point I am trying to make. We have all experienced captivity of some sort. Perhaps we have never been behind physical bars, but we have experienced jails of captivity within ourselves. Some have gratefully been locked in a cell of love. Others have been held behind bars of hatred, bitterness, or sin.

This kind of imprisonment doesn't happen overnight. Doors are closed through a continual process of allowing things in our lives that should not be there or by shutting things out of our lives that should be there. What we need to consider are some of the places where this confinement is allowed to start.

## Part 2: A Battleground

A neuron is a specialized cell in the human brain responsible for communication between the different regions. One neuron has the capacity to send out thousands of signals every second. Multiply this by the millions of neurons and connections in the brain and you can quickly see that there is a lot of thought activity going on every second of every day.

Some of this thought is subconscious—our brain interacting with our body to make sure that our lungs continue to breathe, our heart continues to beat, and our immune system responds to imminent threats. But much of this neuron activity is also conscious thoughts—the 'voices' inside our head that allow us to think and to make decisions. It is these 'voices' that we can either listen to or ignore.

These conscious thoughts are what we want to now look at together. Eugene Peterson paraphrases Paul's statement to the church in Corinth like this:

> *We use our powerful God-tools for smashing warped philosophies, tearing down barriers erected against the truth of God, fitting every loose thought and emotion and impulse into the structure of life shaped by Christ. Our tools are ready at hand for clearing the ground of every obstruction and building lives of obedience into maturity.*
> ~ *2 Corinthians 10:5-6 (MSG)*

These 'loose thoughts' can sometimes cause obstructions in our life. One here and one there—they often escape our attention. But let's think about the verse in 2 Chronicles that we opened this chapter with. If we let certain thoughts come into battle with us, we will lose. We hang on to them a little too long, allowing them to get stored away and retrieved from time to time, consciously and unconsciously. These loose thoughts begin to gain ground, multiplying themselves into thought patterns, which grow into actions and eventually become habits. The battle of our mind needs to go straight back to the front line of disallowing these small 'loose thoughts' to continue.

I just got back from the dentist. I spent a horrendous 45 minutes (which felt like 18 hours) undergoing an intense scraping of my teeth accompanied by a kindhearted lecture that if I flossed a little more the process of cleaning off the gunk would be a little easier. But that's why I go to the dentist—twice a year I allow myself to suffer through the pain of scraping away the junk that shouldn't be on the front of my teeth. It hurts, but I know in the long run it's a whole lot better than letting it all build up and lead to a host of other oral issues.

> If we let certain thoughts come into battle with us, we will lose. If we hang on a little too long, a foothold will be gained against us.

I am sure you can tell where I am going with this. As we dive into this discussion on taking thoughts captive, I want you to remember that nothing happens overnight. The thought patterns we deal with are often a host of small things that we have let accumulate. It's the little things that we want to pay close attention to. If we keep 'scraping' our hearts regularly, those little things won't build up to be the big problems that seem to be in many of our lives. Likewise, if we do have some major issues, it may take a few 'scrapings' to get things back to where we want them to be.

## CREATING THAT WHICH CONSUMES US...

Sometimes we have lost the reality of just how powerful thoughts can be. We wonder why we have trouble with temptation in our lives, but we are not fighting the battle of those loose thoughts tumbling around in our brain. Instead, we allow wrong thoughts to walk into battle with us and wonder why we cannot seem to gain victory over key areas of our life.

Many of us think that if we are tempted to do something, it's too late—if it is in our mind, it is going to have to be put into action. This is not true at all. A temptation is simply a thought, and it is up to you what happens to that thought. It is what we do with each thought that ultimately sets us on either the path of restoration or the path of destruction.

> How we handle each thought is what ultimately sets us on either the path of restoration or the path of destruction.

Henri Nouwen is an internationally renowned priest and author. In his book, *The Wounded Healer*, he retells a parable that originated in ancient India about four sons of royalty. The brothers went out to each find a 'specialty'. After a while, they reconvened to share with one another what they had learned.

> "I have mastered a science," said the first, "which makes it possible for me, if I have nothing but a piece of bone of some creature, to create straightaway the flesh that goes with it."
>
> "I," said the second, "know how to grow that creature's skin and hair if there is flesh on its bones."
>
> The third said, "I am able to create its limbs if I have flesh, the skin, and the hair." "And I," concluded the fourth, "know how to give life to that creature if its form is complete..."
>
> Thereupon the four brothers went into the jungle to find a piece of bone so that they could demonstrate their specialties. As fate would have it, the bone they found was a lion's....One added flesh to the bone, the second grew hide and hair, the third completed it with matching limbs, and the fourth gave the lion life.
>
> Shaking its heavy mane, the ferocious beast arose...and jumped on his creators. He killed them all and vanished contentedly into the jungle.[21]

I think this story is a fitting proverb for looking at our thought life. Thoughts can be generated within us or can come from an outside source. We have this amazing ability, however, to control where they go regardless of how they have surfaced. The reality we need to face is that where we put these thoughts is the ultimate make-or-break point.

This is really where the battle lies. If we allow certain thoughts to take root, they will eventually devour us.

> **We have the ability to control where our thoughts go once they surface. If we allow certain thoughts to take root, they will eventually devour us.**

There are steps involved in setting up any habit, whether that habit is good or bad. The four brothers in the story had to work together to create something—there was an order to their formation. Likewise, with us, there is an order to what becomes our life. Look at the following flowchart:

Thoughts → Desires → Actions → Habits → Lifestyle

Think of each thought in your mind as a bone that you are capable of turning into a living creature. If you could determine the type of bone before you started the process, you would know what the end result would be. In our lives, it works the same way. Certain thoughts and thought patterns will result in certain actions, whether we want them to or not. If we can recognize the thoughts, we can stop this process before they get beyond our control. In other words, we need to recognize a lion's bone before we create something that will devour us.

I believe that a big part of our problem when dealing with the challenges of the process of purity is that we focus on the actions more than on the initial thoughts. It is extremely hard to stop an action if the thought pattern has already been put into place to give life to that action. That is why the battle must go to the beginning of the flowchart I have outlined—capturing the thoughts before they turn into desires. We will deal with the action side of this process in another chapter, but I believe if we can get things handled on this frontline, the battle becomes much easier.

> Dealing with the bone itself is much easier than dealing with the lion that stands before you.

I teach piano and tutor math in my spare time. Most students who have been with me for any amount of time have had to suffer through one of my 'it's all about what you're thinking' lectures. Henry Ford once said, "If you think you can do a thing or think you can't do a thing, you're right."[22] I often quote that to my students before they try to show me a piece or a task they have mastered. If you approach a task thinking you are going to fail at it, no doubt you will. The action has already been given life through the thought pattern. You must believe that you are going to accomplish what you have set out to accomplish. It's like this in everything we do.

> **A big part of the problem when dealing with the process of purity is that we focus on the actions more than on the initial thoughts. We need to recognize a lion's bone before we create something that will devour us.**

Saint Augustine said, "Men go abroad to wonder at the heights of mountains, at the huge waves of the sea, at the long courses of the rivers, at the vast compass of the ocean, at the circular motions of the stars, and they pass by themselves without wondering."[23] Perhaps it's time we studied ourselves a little bit more. Understanding what we are capable of becomes the first step. The second step is acting on this knowledge in a manner that is going to have the outcome we are looking for. Knowing we are capable of creating an animal with our hands does us no good if the animal we create devours us. It's the same with our thought patterns.

## Who's Captivating Who?

It's funny the twists and turns the road of life can take. Sometimes we need to relearn a few things along the way.

Perhaps it's time we studied ourselves a little more. Understanding what we are capable of becomes the first step.

The things we know to be foundational in life can be overlooked because they have always been there. We take the cornerstones of our spiritual lives for granted until we see what we have built beginning to crumble due to their disregard. Truly, time and neglect, if allowed to walk hand-in-hand, collapse these cornerstones and compromise our foundation.

I have attended many leadership workshops (and taught them myself) in which it has been warned that one comment made in a negative tone can destroy the effect of a thousand positive comments. Negativity breeds negativity. In our human fragility, it is easy to get caught up in a pessimistic view of reality.

That's why I have a hard time hanging around people who have negative, critical tendencies. These are not folks I tend to allow into the deeper parts of my soul. Why? Because I am a person who tries very hard to see the good in people. I try hard to encourage people in their walk with God and in their purpose here on this earth—that's one of the foundations of CPM Enterprises and a core belief of mine. I personally find that negativity drains the life out of me, and I know that I can very easily follow suit, so I try to guard my mind against it.

Well, that got me thinking about my thinking (hmmm—my education degree is flying back into my face—that would be called 'metacognition' for those of you who care). I have been actively working on guarding my mind against negative thoughts.

But this is only one area of thought, one aspect of life. Let's read again the words from Paul that opened this chapter.

> *We demolish arguments and every pretension that sets itself up against the knowledge of God, and we take captive* every thought *to make it obedient to Christ.*
> ~ *2 Corinthians 10:5 (NIV, emphasis mine)*

*Every thought.* Take every thought captive. Not just the thoughts of negativity, but the thoughts of righteousness, thoughts of impurity, thoughts of malice, and thoughts of blessing. Every thought that we allow into our mind must be taken captive—must be caught and checked out before we allow it to do anything else.

**Every thought. Not just the thoughts of negativity, but the thoughts of righteousness, impurity, malice, and blessing.**

We have heard it all before. My youth pastor would consistently drill this phrase into my brain when I was a teen, to the point where it became a joke. I am grateful, however, that he invested the time to do this. Everything that enters into our brain must be able to pass the Philippians 4:8 test:

> *...Fix your thoughts on what is true and honorable and right. Think about things that are pure and lovely and admirable. Think about things that are excellent and worthy of praise.*

When a thought enters our mind, we must run through the above checklist. Is this thought honourable and right? Is it pure and worthy of praise? If it passes the checklist, then we let the thought pass into storage. If it doesn't, we discard it and think of it no more. We consciously say that this thought is not permitted in our brain, and we pray for strength to turn our minds toward those thoughts that do pass the test.

In the writing of this book, I didn't need to look up Philippians 4:8. Rather, I copied it from a poster taped to the wall by my desk. I placed it there so that it would be a constant reminder of the necessity of testing every thought. Over the years, I have often allowed sticky notes to go over top of it—it has blended into the atmosphere of the room in such a way that sometimes I find myself looking at it without looking at it. That can be a dangerous place to be.

> But here's the real 'captivating thought'
> that we all need to hear:
> It is not a question of captivity,
> but rather a question of who is going to be the captive.

Either we take each of our thoughts captive and disallow those thoughts that fall short of the Philippians 4:8 test, or those thoughts take us captive. If we let our guard down, we suddenly find ourselves doing the very things we do not want to do (see Romans 7:15). I can tell you this from firsthand experience, and I am sure you can relate as well. If we let our thoughts run away with us, we find that our actions quickly fall in line with those thought patterns. Repeat the action enough times, and you are now dealing with a habit that will bring regret and shame.

> **Either we take each of our thoughts captive and disallow those thoughts that fall short of the Philippians 4:8 test, or those thoughts take us captive.**

You have been there too. Perhaps you have let bitterness well up inside you and then found yourself lashing out at a loved one for no particular reason. Or maybe you have allowed thoughts of that coworker in the office next to you to go too far, and now you've gotten yourself in a tangled mess. Maybe you've let negativity reach the point where your temper flares and your family gets hurt.

There will always be captivity in this life, but we can determine who is going to be the captive. Either we control our thoughts or we let our thoughts control us. It is up to us. And let me tell you, the former is much harder than the latter. But in the end, we are left with a cornerstone that will not crumble.

Why is the former so much harder? Because it's a never-ending battle. We have already talked about the thousands of thoughts that go through our heads each second. That's a lot of testing to do, and often we just get tired of the fight. But just as wrongful thoughts lead to wrongful actions, correct thoughts will lead to correct actions. I believe it is possible to get into the habit of captivating our thoughts. It can even become as natural as breathing.

> *For when your faith is tested, your endurance has a chance to grow. So let it grow, for when your endurance is fully developed, you will be strong in character and ready for anything.*
> ~ James 1:3-4

You *can* be strong in character and ready for anything! It starts at the level of your thoughts. You feel unworthiness creep into your mind. You sit on the thought, and then wonder why you find yourself overindulging in that leftover cake at 3:00am. You hang for just a moment on a thought that suggests what your flesh desires instead of what God desires, and you find yourself dismounting the altar of sacrifice and giving in to the very thing you've grown to hate. If we can train ourselves to stop when we realize we are holding a lion's bone, this process of purity that we are trying to live out becomes much more manageable.

Can God change a person's nature? Yes, but it often requires a lot of little-by-little steps, many of them forced because they go against the 'lions' we have already created. Part of my job as a school teacher is to get my students to do what they do not want to do so that someday they will be what they always wanted to be. It's the same in life. We need to go against our human nature because, in our spiritual mind, we can see the bigger picture. God's grace is there when we fall, and we will from time to time. Remember that this is not an overnight transformation. His strength will continue to be there for us to take that next step.

> God changes our nature through a lot of little-by-little steps. Never forget that God's grace is there when we fall.

It must start at the level of our thoughts. Who is being taken captive in your mind? Are your thoughts captivating you, or are you captivating them? It takes a lot of baby steps to win the battle for our minds, but we all need to start somewhere. Take heart from pillars of the early church like Saint Paul and Saint Augustine who had to come to this realization as well.

God takes each and every one of us where we are at and draws us along a little further, a little closer to the realization of who we are and what we have been created to be. Take a close look at the bone in front of you before you let your creative power loose.

Captivating thoughts.
But who is being the captive?
With God's grace, we can win this battle for our mind.

# Chapter 8: Exterior Battle Lines

Don't become so well-adjusted to your culture that you fit into it without even thinking. Instead, fix your attention on God. You'll be changed from the inside out.

~Romans 12:2a (MSG)

y regular study Bible has a commentary posted at the bottom of each page for the majority of the verses at the top. I have always marvelled at the commentary note that tells me there was a span of several years between one recorded verse and the next. It makes me try to imagine what happened between the lines. For instance, after Saul's Damascus road encounter with Jesus, he "stayed with believers in Damascus for a few days" (Acts 9:19b). Seven verses later we are told of him arriving in Jerusalem (9:26). Behind the scenes, however, we know through other historical records that Paul traveled to Arabia and stayed there for three years in the middle of this biblical narrative. For some reason or another, Luke had a chronological pause in the telling of his story.

This chapter represents a personal pause for me in the writing of this book. There have been several months between my penning the thoughts on captivation that you read just moments ago and the opening up of this current chapter. Part of it has been the responsibilities of other jobs and demands on my time. Part of it may also have been a reluctance to sit face to face with this issue of external battle lines. Winning the battle for your mind is tough enough, let alone trying to curb actions that are not in keeping with living a pure life.

As I sit and write out my thoughts, there is a large part of me that feels I have no right to do so, because people reading it will consider me an authority in this matter. In many ways it feels hypocritical of me to tell you about facing your exterior battle lines head on, to chat with you about the practical applications of living out our process of purity—our reasonable act of worship. I feel somewhat two-faced writing down these thoughts when I, at times, consider myself to be so inadequate in the process. The battle gets tiring, and the fight sometimes doesn't feel worth it.

Having God mould and shape us into the people he has destined us to be is not a passive action. We have a part to play, and it's time to look at some of those practical applications. I want to take some time to deal with these applications in the next two chapters. Please know, however, that I am taking this journey with you as one walking alongside of you, not as one who claims to have already arrived.

> **Having God mould and shape us into the people he has destined us to be is not a passive action.**
> **We have a part to play.**

At the end of the day, we have a battle that we are called to actively fight. It matters not how we feel about that battle at any given moment; it is our job to fight it anyway. Christ will be by our side—we need not fear. He will strengthen us in our walk as we move our feet forward. We have reason to be encouraged, but we must never forget that it is our choice to make.

It is *our* job to live out this process of purity, not God's. It is *our* job to see the warning signs and to flee from them. It is *our* job to not let ourselves get too comfortable in the culture we live in, realizing that this is not our permanent home. It is *our* job to, "let God transform you into a new person by changing the way you think" (Romans 12:2b). Did you catch the subtlety of that verse? We allow God to transform us *as we change the way we think*. God's not going to do that part for us.

Paul tells us in 1 Corinthians 10:13 that God will never allow a temptation in our life where he does not also provide a way out. It is our job to take the way out that has been provided. Often we sit and look at the open door and wonder why God isn't pushing us through and 'saving us' from this thing we cannot bear. All the while, he is simply waiting for us to get off our blessed assurance and walk through the door ourselves! This is where we need to be proactive.

We have already discussed the battle for our mind—the real beginning of this transformation from within. I talked about our thoughts as the frontline of battle. If we can begin to control our thought patterns, we can begin to win some of these battles before inner issues give birth to outer actions. Changing the way we think allows God the opportunity to do an inward renovation that will strengthen our life-long journey through this process of purity.

However, while we still have breath in our lungs, there is another aspect to the drawing of our battle lines. The reality of life is that we have already allowed wrong thoughts to form into wrong actions. Most of us are already dealing with habits of lust, short tempers, fantasy, pride, self-righteousness, negative self image, and gluttony—these outward actions must be addressed if we are going to see success in our daily walk.

Now we need to deal with the fight in the area of our actions—the battle lines that need to be formed on the exterior. These battles are often the most difficult ones to fight and the easiest ones to give in to. Each battle, won or lost, will have an ultimate effect on how the war for purity is played out in our lives.

> **The reality of life is that we have already allowed wrong thoughts to form into wrong actions. We must address these outward actions if we hope to see success.**

We have the ability to live a life that is fruitful, to walk a journey that's successful, and to have relationships that are meaningful and fulfilling. The roadblocks that seem to be in our way, though, are the battles

Part 2: A Battleground

that vie for our attention. We consistently need to fight against the innate desire to step off the altar of self sacrifice. If we learn how to fight, we can win some of these battles while we still have life on this earth. I don't want to just make it into heaven by the skin of my teeth and the grip of God's grace. I want to be able to walk into heaven and hear my Saviour say that he is proud of the battles that I fought while I lived out this first stage of eternal life.

> Do you want to just make it to heaven by the skin of your teeth and the grip of God's grace, or do you want to be able to walk into heaven and hear your Saviour say that he is proud?

In order to experience success in these battles, I believe there are some keys. To fight effectively on the outside requires a hard look on the inside, just as Peterson's paraphrase of Paul's words opening up this chapter imply. Really, it is this inward revolution that we have been dealing with throughout our entire journey together. Let's now dig a little deeper.

## GETTING TO THE ROOT...

I am not much into self-reflection. When I was going through my education degree, self reflection was the buzzword of the day. Every activity we did in that two-year program ended with some sort of inner contemplation. We would often be asked to do a small group wrap-up where we discussed with a partner all the realizations about ourselves and about our practices that we had learned through some introspective activity.

Reflection was one of my least favourite words—I got so sick and tired of hearing professors use it. We live in a world where people don't really want to stop and reflect on what is going on deep within them. Compelling ourselves to take an inward look at our lives will force us to see things that we would rather not admit are there.

If you are trying to get rid of dandelions in your backyard, you will quickly learn that popping the head and stem off is simply not enough. Within a day or two, there is at least one more in the same spot, flourishing like nothing happened. Why? Because you need to take out the root. As long as the root still has an anchor in the ground, the plant will grow back time and time again.

It's the same in our own lives. Any outward sinful action is really the manifestation of some inward issue—there is always an interior root to an exterior problem. We might be able to curb the outward action for a period of time, but the root will eventually manifest itself again. In order to begin winning the surface battles of actions and habits, we need to dig down to the root and deal with the underlying problems.

> There is always an interior root to an exterior problem. In order to begin winning the surface battles of actions and habits, we need to dig down to the root and deal with the underlying problems.

What is beneath the surface of your life? What is inside those dark caverns of your heart that you try so hard to avoid looking into? I believe there are two rooms in our heart where the rest of our problems and struggles are birthed. These rooms are painful to deal with, but facing them with honest eyes and the willingness to clean them out is absolutely necessary if we want to walk through this process of purity in victory more than in defeat. Let's take a look at these two rooms together.

## Lack of Trust

Written on the door of the first room is *Lack of Trust*. When all is said and done, we struggle through this life because we are trying to do things in our own strength. Simply stated, we are scared to give over the control of our lives to someone else. Oswald Chambers once said that "abandonment means to refuse yourself the luxury of asking any questions."[24] I believe true worship is worship that is done in a state of abandonment. True worship involves letting go of whatever it is that we are holding on to and letting the questions subside.

For many of us, we struggle with a particular habit simply because God is asking us to step out and trust him. Why is trust such an issue for us? Why can't we just allow God to do what he wants to do and trust him that he has our best interests in mind? Adam's lack of trust ended with the eating of forbidden fruit and the resulting entrance of sin and death upon the entire human race. Abraham's lack of trust ended in a concubine's son whose offspring would forever be at war with the nation of Israel. Judas' lack of trust ended with a rope around his neck instead of becoming an influential leader in Christ's new kingdom. Your lack of trust ends up with that office affair, or that new car you didn't really need and couldn't really afford, or that escape mechanism to which you turn when your world doesn't make sense. The outward action may be different for each of us, but the inward root is the same.

We must learn to trust. We must believe that God has our best interests in his mind. If we can come to this realization, I truly believe the things that ensnare us will begin to lose their grip. This isn't going to change overnight, but if you don't start with one baby step, you'll never get anywhere. No matter how long a journey is, it will never begin until a step in that direction is taken. What small step can you take today? For a moment, examine yourself. Write down one thing you can do this coming week that will be a step in the right direction for your trust to develop. Now commit yourself to doing it.

## The Spirit of Demanding

The second room of our heart is closely connected to the first. On its door is written *The Spirit of Demanding*. Ever since we came into this world, we have demanded our own way. Sometimes it expresses itself through pride, sometimes through control issues, or even through sarcastic comments. Some seasoned veterans have been able to hide it under a guise of ministry, volunteerism or philanthropy. Within each of us, however, a demanding spirit is still there, and it needs to be dealt with.

> God invades the deepest recesses of our deceitful heart to ruthlessly expose what needs to be changed. His *acceptance* of us on the basis of Calvary and His *understanding* of our hurt provide the context for His work in our heart, but relentless *exposure* of our arrogant demandingness begins the healing. As we learn to recognize, hate, and abandon our demanding spirit and to entrust the Lord with our deepest longings, we clean the inside of the cup and dish.
>
> ~ Larry Crabb[25]

What are you demanding from God? Maybe all you want is happiness. Perhaps you want to find true fulfillment. Maybe all you have ever desired was a godly home and successful children. Whether the requests sound good or bad, the root needs to be exposed. Who are we to ask God for anything? Who are we to demand our own way?

> *Who is this that questions my wisdom with such ignorant words?...Where were you when I laid the foundations of the earth? Tell me, if you know so much....Who defined the boundaries of*

> *the sea as it burst from the womb?...Have you ever commanded the morning to appear?...Where does the light come from and where does the darkness go? Can you take it to its home? Do you know how to get there? But of course you know all this! For you were born before it was all created, and you are so very experienced!*
>
> ~ Job 38:2-12, 19-21

Do you get the picture? Job did. Job realized that in the middle of his own suffering, even in the middle of his own righteousness, there was an underlying issue of a lack of trust and a demanding spirit. Be willing to face these same rooms in your own heart. Once we get to the root, the surface level battles cease to be the failures that they so often tend to be.

**What are you demanding from God? Whether the requests sound good or bad, the root needs to be exposed. Who are we to ask God for anything?**

Take another minute of reflection (oops, I said that word!). In what ways are you demanding something from God that you really have no right to demand? Stop and have a conversation with your creator. Be willing to ask God to come in and clean the inside of your cup and dish.[26]

God requires a change from us that begins on the inside and works its way out. If we don't deal with these rooms in our hearts, we will find ourselves fitting in and conforming to a world that is not our home. Cleaning out these rooms is a vital step in the process of allowing God to transform our minds.

## Knowing Your Triggers...

No soldier walks into a battle zone without some basic preparation. In any combat, we want to know ahead of time the strategies our enemy will use. This way, we will not be ambushed.

The same rings true in the spiritual realm. It's important to know your triggers when you are trying to win this battle of purity. These triggers are the things in your life that make you more susceptible to attack while you try to be the living sacrifice that God has called you and destined you to be.

> There will always be times when the battle is fiercer and the temptation is greater. If we can see those times coming up, we will be able to guard ourselves against them.

There will always be times when the battle is fiercer and the temptation is greater. If we can see those times coming up, we will be able to guard ourselves against them and perhaps have an easier time getting through the battle victoriously.

The following are some key triggers that you need to guard against. I know from experience that when any of these triggers appear in my life, I often stumble and falter in my walk. If we can be proactive about their appearance, perhaps we can protect ourselves a little better.

1. Fatigue

We are notorious for trying to get too many things done in the run of a day. Between working full-time as a teacher, running CPM with its three separate divisions, and then trying to stay connected with people and relationships, I tend to crash. It is in this period of physical and spiritual weariness that the temptation to walk off the path of purity becomes much greater.

We are already aware of the warning signs. Hectic schedules and deadlines with family and ministry will never go away. However, we can combat fatigue by not letting these things gain so much control over our lives. Time management and priority-setting are integral to godly living.

The world is not going to come to a crashing halt if you take a break. Take a day and go for a walk. Take a vacation and get out of your usual element. Take some time to just be with your family. Commit time to fasting and prayer. Whatever it looks like for you, take the time to rejuvenate yourself before fatigue sets in and you end up dealing with the consequences.

Our physical self and our spiritual self are not separate from each other. Eating right, exercising daily, and getting the proper amount of rest will help us stay spiritually fit because our physical self will be taken care of. Stop fatigue before it happens. Surface battles then become much easier to fight.

2. Transitions

A change in your job, a change in your schedule, a change in your relationships, a change in your location—change causes stress. I am not a person who deals well with change. My brother always jokes with me and tells me I take too long to process things, but it's partly because I go through a lot of mental battles when periods of change come at me.

Maybe you are one of those people who thrive on change. You love to seize the moment and the opportunity that lies before you. I'll rise to the challenge as well, but not without some inner battles and temptations to fight along the way. I suspect many of you are the same. Whether we want to admit it or not, we are people who thrive on routine and predictability. We don't question the rising of the sun every morning or the passing of the seasons throughout a year. We understand the rhythm and routine of nature around us and we cherish that same rhythm within ourselves. So, when something comes about to change that rhythm, we become easy targets for satan's attacks.

Please listen to what I am saying. There is nothing wrong with change—it is both healthy and necessary to go through periods of transition within your life. Don't run away from change—embrace it. Only be aware that change can bring with it an unsettling in your soul. This will often tempt you to revert to the familiar low road when it comes to the journey of being a living sacrifice. You may be tempted to get off that altar instead of allowing God to complete the change he wants to complete in your character and lifestyle. Be encouraged, take heart, and stay on the altar.

**Triggers to Be Aware Of:**
1. Fatigue
2. Transitions
3. Situations Outside Your Control

3. Situations Outside of Your Control

A family member gets diagnosed with cancer; you get laid off at the local plant; your child turns his back on God—there are always situations that arise in our lives over which we have no control. When these situations appear, the temptation to sin becomes much greater.

When the world is spinning around us, we want something that we can control. We need to be able to dominate something in the hopes of giving ourselves a false sense of security. The result is often some sort of moral judgment lapse in the area of purity. We find ourselves up eating junk food late at night, simply because we can make the choice to do so. We find our tempers flaring at our children only because they are in a position where they have to listen to us. We find ourselves gossiping about the neighbour down the road because it gives us a sense of being above them.

When situations arise that are out of our control, we must learn to trust in God. Trust that his hand is guiding us, whether we can tangibly see it or not.

What does this sort of trust look like? If we get laid off, should we sit on the couch waiting for the phone to ring when our feet haven't hit the pavement to find employment? Trusting does not mean we take a passive role. I think it is important to make that distinction here.

Remember that situations outside of our control are bound to come. When these situations do occur, be proactive about staying on the path of purity. Know that temptation will be greater during these times than in times of peace and tranquility. Be on your guard concerning those areas of purity to which you are most susceptible.

This is not by any means meant to be an exhaustive list of the warning signs and triggers to watch for, but I believe they are key ones. Just like in the mathematical game of chess, planning your strategies ahead of time will allow you to be ready for any move your opponent may throw at you. Decide to live your life on the offence instead of only on the defence.

> Just like in the mathematical game of chess, planning your strategies ahead of time will allow you to be ready. We must live our lives on the offence instead of only on the defence.

## Not Even a Hint...

Compromise has been said to be the glue that holds relationships together. It's the key to healthy marriages, strong business partners, and lasting friendships. In the area of purity, however, compromise is a four-letter word. The Bible carries with it a stern warning about compromise:

> *But among you there must not be even a hint of sexual immorality, or of any kind of impurity, or of greed, because these are improper for God's holy people.*
> ~ *Ephesians 5:3 (NIV)*

Those are harsh words. Anyone willing to take an honest look at his or her life will have to admit that there is at least a hint of one of those things somewhere within. Why is Paul being so tough on us? Where's the gracious God who is slow to anger and abounding in compassion?

It's not a big deal...
It's not hurting anyone...
Surely this tiny area of my life doesn't make that much
of a difference...
One little compromise won't do that much damage...

I am sure these same thoughts ran through the minds of three young men named Hananiah, Mishael, and Azariah. Doesn't sound familiar? Maybe, if you're a VeggieTales fan, you would know them as Rack, Shack, and Benny. Otherwise, you can check out the full meal deal in Daniel 3. These three Hebrew men were told to bow before the golden statue King Nebuchadnezzar had built. It's not like they were being picked on—all the people of Babylon were given the same orders. The nation was also warned that the punishment for noncompliance was death-by-fire.

No one would have blamed them if they had bowed down. In fact, I have no doubt there were other Hebrew men within the walls of Babylon that the Bible does not mention. Perhaps they took the bow, justifying that they would be a much better witness to the Babylonian people alive then dead. Surely God would overlook their small compromise for the greater good—surely God would be able to see that their hearts were not in tune with their actions.

But these three boys stood by the 'not even a hint' principle. They willingly decided it would be better to go to their graves than to compromise their standards. The result was a show of fireworks that were out of this world, with all of the glory going to God.

> Even the smallest thing that we allow in our lives that is not under the control of the Holy Spirit is completely sufficient to account for spiritual confusion, and spending all of our time thinking about it will still never make it clear. Spiritual confusion can only be conquered through obedience.
>
> ~ Oswald Chambers[27]

Tim MacDonald is the vice chairman of CPM's board of directors and a close friend of mine. He served as my youth pastor during my teenage years. I can always remember him telling a version of the following story to get the 'not even a hint' principle ingrained into our brain cells.

Imagine for a moment that a company mass produces oven-baked, soft, chewy chocolate chip cookies. Each batch will make 5000 cookies that will be packaged up and shipped to stores across the country. Imagine if a worker put one teaspoon of dog doo into that batch of 5000 cookies. The chance that this trace amount of canine compost in your individual snack would affect your health is very small...but would you knowingly eat it? Of course not—that small hint of impurity is enough to spoil the whole batch.

> *Your boasting is not good. Don't you know that a little yeast works through the whole batch of dough?*
>
> ~ *1 Corinthians 5:6 (NIV)*

It's not enough to say that we are sold out to God 90% of the time. If you are in a marriage relationship, do you think your partner would be satisfied with your faithfulness 90% of the time? What if you were faithful for 9 years and 11 months out of every 10 years? That's pretty consistent, right? Is that enough to make a marriage relationship survive and flourish? Of course not! By the very sanctity of the marriage bed, it requires 100% devotion. The same is true of our relationship with God. God is a jealous God, and he requires 100% of us.

> It's not enough to say that we are sold out to God 90% of the time. God is a jealous God, and he requires 100% of us.

Search your heart. What hints of impurity lie within its walls? Be committed to giving God 100% of yourself. Anything less is not enough.

Roots. Triggers. Hints. At the surface level of actions and habits, the knowledge of these three areas becomes vitally important. Don't rush the moment. Search your own life and allow God to speak to you in his still, small voice. What is he saying to you right now? What do you need to say to him?

# Chapter 9: The Battle Continues

We are human, but we don't wage war with human plans and methods.

~2 Corinthians 10:3

I have told you all this so that you may have peace in me. Here on earth you will have many trials and sorrows. But take heart, because I have overcome the world.

~John 16:33

Our history books are full of famous combat accounts—the Battle of Waterloo, the atomic bombing of Japan, the Battle of Hastings. History depicts the unfolding of legendary quarrels from the eyes of both the winners and the losers. Also recounted within the pages of historical records are wars that have been fought—the 'meta battles' that have shaped nations and the very demographics of the earth we now live in. You can read about WWI and WWII, the Cold War, the War of 1812, the French Revolution—every nationality has a story to relate to its new generation about an ultimate price that was paid.

So what's the difference between a battle and a war? History talks of both, but makes a distinction between the two. A battle has a set beginning, end, and outcome. It is a conflict between two parties that is won by one side and lost by the other. A war is the bigger picture. It is a series of battles fought collectively and over a longer period of time. The opponent who wins the war is not necessarily the one who takes the most battles, but rather the one who prevails in the final battle.

Our Christian walk through this process of purity is a succession of battles that need to be fought. We face many trials, temptations, and tests that end in either a win or loss. This chapter continues to look at some of the strategies—lines of attack and lines of defence—that we need to bring with us into battle in order to see favourable outcomes.

As we study the battle lines, however, we should keep the bigger picture in the forefront of our minds. If we have made the choice to follow Christ with our whole heart, the ultimate victory of this war has already been decided.

If we are sincerely fighting these battles, we *will* see ultimate victory. This can be such a frustrating statement when you're in the middle of the fray and seem to be losing more often than you are winning. Don't lose sight of this fact—God is shaping us *through* the journey. God continues to form us with each individual battle if we will allow him to do so. The war, on the other hand, has already been won through Christ's death on the cross and resurrection. Take a minute and let these words encourage you. The war has already been won! You are going to make it through this process—thanks be to God! Stop for a minute, and thank him for all that he has done in your life.

**Never forget that the ultimate victory has already been decided. Never lose sight of the fact that God is shaping you through the journey.**

We may not see this final victory played out in our lives until our bodies have been completely transformed on the other side of eternity. But we will see it. This has been promised to us, and it is a promise we can rest in. If we learn to stand upon this pledge, the individual battles will be more easily won. Fighting in a war that you know can be won gives you the courage, the strength, and the discipline to carry on when desire and will are not there.

The journey through this process is much easier if we remember that the battles we face and fight are for a war that has ultimately been won. Our goal is to stay within the boundary lines of the winning side. It is the outcome of each individual battle that will determine the quality of our spiritual life while we walk this earth in its present form.

Let's continue on our journey and look at some more lines of defence and offence.

## HOW BAD DO YOU WANT IT?

Our desire for air is a funny thing. We don't really think about how strong an affinity we have for the substance until that substance is no longer available. Any one of us who has taken a dive into a deep pool of water has felt it. In the depths beneath the surface of the pool, we have a desire to breathe. If we open our mouths, there will be no air to take in. We suddenly realize just how badly we want that air. A strong desire makes us swim with passion and fierceness to the surface so we can obtain what our body craves. As we break through the canopy of water and fill our lungs with glorious oxygen, our racing heart begins to subside and our appreciation dwindles until such a time when air is once again needed but not available.

I once watched a stunt man who spent a week in a water bubble with a supply of air. To end his act, he was tied up and cut off from his air supply inside the oversized fish bowl. No doubt his desire for air was a key factor in his ability to loose the chains that were around him—he had a life or death reason to succeed.

> **There comes a time in living a life of purity when we simply have to decide how seriously we want it.**

There are chains around us as well. Chains of habit, sin, and compromise wrap themselves around us and constrict our movements. We are faced with a life or death reason to be motivated as well...but are we? Is the motivation really there?

There comes a time in living a life of purity when we simply have to decide how seriously we want it. We get tired of the fight—we get tired of taking the high road when the lower elevation seems to offer an easier journey. Sometimes, when we reach this stage in our battle, it boils down to asking one tough question.

How bad do you want this life of purity?

What is it worth to you? Sure, God will be there for you in your struggles, but he is not going to take them away. God has given us a free will. Simply put, there is absolutely nothing he will force us to do or not do. It comes down to your own inner searching and questioning—how bad do you want this?

It's got to be your decision. It's got to be your own resolve.

> ...I keep working toward that day when I will finally be all that Christ Jesus saved me for and wants me to be. No, dear brothers and sisters, I am still not all I should be, but I am focusing all my energies on this one thing: Forgetting the past and looking forward to what lies ahead. I strain to reach the end of the race and receive the prize for which God, through Christ Jesus, is calling us up to heaven.
> ~ Philippians 3:12-14

Do you see the action words in this passage?

"I keep working..."<br>
"I am focusing all my energies..."<br>
"I strain to reach the end of the race..."

This is tiring stuff. Paul doesn't use any fluff in his words. But he knew how badly he wanted to live out this life of purity. I firmly believe that on some days it was his own determination that made him fight the good fight.

There comes a time when we have to realize that 'the devil made me do it' is no longer a valid excuse. No longer can we blame our parents for the lifestyle we are living. It's time to physically walk away from temptation. In a nutshell, we must train our bodies to live purely. Just as an athlete subjects her body to various forms of pain in order to achieve her goal, so we must do the same.

Sometimes, we just have to say no to ourselves. No one else is going to do it for us.

It is like our affinity for air. How much do I want to live a life of purity? What is it worth to me? Is it worth the sacrifice? These are real questions we have to come to grips with. If we do not, we will continue on this roller coaster for the rest of our lives, cycling up and down, living a defeated and divided life.

> **It's time to physically walk away from temptation. Sometimes we just have to say no to ourselves. No one else is going to do it for us.**

It comes down to a choice, and we must choose to fight. We in the western world don't really think about that. We want to *feel* spiritual. We want to have our charismatic goose bumps and say that everything is okay. We have discussed much, and still have more to cover, but having the knowledge alone will not help our fight if the desire to fight is not there.

Ask yourself the tough questions.

> We only get one kick at this can called life.
> What direction do you want your kick to go?
> How bad do you want it?

It's okay to admit that your desire is not where it should be. It's okay to admit that sometimes you don't want to fight. It's okay to admit that sometimes you don't want to succeed. You can recognize your lack of desire and use it as an opportunity—as another plan of attack. Ask God for his strength, and ask God to light that spark that is deep within you. If you are willing to ask, God is willing to fan that spark back into a flame. God is willing to align your desires with his if you will let him change you.

## LIFE THROUGH STARVATION...

I sit here at my computer with study books around me and a cold cup of coffee on my desk. Deep within my body is a knot that releases itself from time to time as a rumbling of my stomach. My body is trying to let me know that it needs food—it's coming up to lunch time and my body knows it. In order for me to stay alive, I will soon need to eat something. This provision will allow my body to create the energy required to keep all my biological systems working properly.

Life exists through cuisine. From the lowest amoebic structure to the most complex of the animal kingdom, all of life is sustained in the same manner. Nutrients are ingested and then broken down and converted into the energy needed to function. If the food supply of a particular organism is cut off, life will eventually cease for that organism. Often, in the ecosystems of the world, the termination of one organism provides a niche for another organism to flourish.

This concept can be applied to our spiritual selves. Picture within yourself two organisms both vying for the nutrients that you provide them. The starvation of one organism will allow for the growth of the other. In a paradoxical setting, life for one comes through the starvation of the other.

The first organism in this competition for survival is the part of you formed by the hand of your creator. It is the God-given potential that is inside of you and longs to be lived out on this earth through a successful journey upon the high road of our purity walk. The rival organism is the component that has been handed down from the father of man, Adam.

> ...For this one man, Adam brought death to many though his sin. But this other man, Jesus Christ, brought forgiveness to many through God's bountiful gift. And the result of God's gracious gift is very different from the result of that one man's sin. For Adam's sin led to condemnation, but we have the free gift of being accepted by God, even though we are guilty of many sins. The sin of this one man, Adam, caused death to rule over us, but all who receive God's wonderful, gracious gift of righteousness will live in triumph over sin and death through this one man, Jesus Christ.
>
> ~ Romans 5:15-17

Your life on earth is really a determination of which one of these organisms is getting fed at any given moment. If you starve the God-given part of you, the Adam-given part will thrive and flourish. Starving the Adam-given part provides the nutrients necessary for the God-given part to grow and abound and for you to experience the triumph over sin and death that Paul talks about.

Both of these organisms cannot grow simultaneously. While he walked the earth, Jesus warned us that a servant is not able to serve two masters—either we will "hate one and love the other, or be devoted to one and despise the other" (Matthew 6:24). One organism's success will always coincide with the other organism's failure.

In order to have life the way we were created to have it, we must starve that which is competing for occupancy space within us. We must cut off the food supply for our sinful self in order to provide the nutrients needed for our godly self to thrive.

How do you starve an organism? You make the choice not to feed it. Joseph had to make the choice. He had control over all that Potiphar owned. And a large house it was, for Potiphar was the personal assistant to Pharaoh. Joseph was the one entrusted to complete all of the business transactions for this wealthy and important man.[28] Potiphar's wife took a shining to young Joseph and invited him to a forbidden bedside rendezvous. I don't imagine for a minute that Potiphar's wife was ugly—I am sure she was the epitome of beauty and seduction, for temptation never comes masked in ugliness. But Joseph stood his ground.

> **Starve the God-given part of you, and the Adam-given part will thrive. Starving the Adam-given part provides the nutrients for the God-given to grow and abound.**

> One day [Joseph] went into the house to attend to his duties, and none of the household servants was inside. She caught him by his cloak and said, "Come to bed with me!" But he left his cloak in her hand and ran out of the house
> ~ Genesis 39: 11-12 (NIV)

Joseph didn't take the time to stop and think about the situation, because he knew that if he entertained the thought, there was a high possibility of the thought becoming an action. He chose instead to starve that part of him and run out of the room. He didn't walk, he didn't even jog—he ran! He made a conscious choice not to feed that part of his nature.

Paul understood this active component of starving his sinful nature as well...

*"Run away from sexual sin!"*
*(1 Corinthians 6:18a)*

*"So, my dear friends, flee from the worship of idols." (1 Corinthians 10:14)*

*"But you...belong to God; so run from all these evil things..." (1 Timothy 6:11)*

*"Run from anything that simulates youthful lust." (2 Timothy 2:22a)*

If you want to begin winning some of these battles in any area of purity that you may face, it is going to involve your active participation in the starving of your sinful nature. Bear in mind that once you decide to cut off the food supply, the cravings for nourishment are bound to get worse. That's why Paul was so graphic in these charges we read above. One small glance at forbidden fruit will cause the growling of a stomach that is hard to ignore. The strategy, then, is to not take the glance.

You know the battles you face. If you want to starve your sinful nature, don't put yourself in a situation that will cause a rumbling in your sinful nature's appetite.

> **Winning some of these battles involves your active participation in the starving of your sinful nature.**

If late night snacks are a habitual routine for you, don't let yourself go to the kitchen in the middle of the night. If internet pornography is the problem at hand, turn your computer off, or at least disconnect yourself from the world wide web. If negative self-talk is your struggle, don't let yourself sit for hours on end listening to the voices inside you vying for your attention.

I went on a one-month fast several years ago where I allowed myself only fruit and uncooked vegetables. I think the hardest

## Part 2: A Battleground

part of the fast was the first week. My body craved meat and I strongly desired something (anything!) to eat that was hot instead of the constant cold fruit that I allowed myself. Even a piece of toast would have felt like heaven! By the time I got to the end of the month, however, my desire for meat was simply not as strong...I didn't crave it anymore. Starving my desire for meat during that first week eventually curbed the desire altogether.

The same rings true in our spiritual walk. If we will take the time to stand our ground, not letting our minds entertain wrong desires, the battle will increasingly get easier. If we will purposefully keep ourselves from situations where we know temptation will occur, victory will be seen more often in our lives. As we cut off the food supply to our sinful nature, the starved desire will begin to lose its lifeblood.

> Run. There is nothing cowardly in running. Take an active role in the starving of your sinful nature. God will give you the strength to continue the battle.

Run. There is nothing cowardly in running. Take an active role in the starving of your sinful nature. Make some room for the flourishing of your God-given potential. No diet is ever easy, because it requires a change in lifestyle. If you have the willingness, God will give you the strength to continue the battle.

## LINE IN THE SAND...

We live in a society that perverts everything to do with our bodies. Jesus commands us to do the exact opposite—to present our bodies as living sacrifices that are holy, acceptable, and pleasing unto him. When dealing with youth and the issue of purity, we often tell our young people that they need to draw a line in the sand and make the sacrifice to never cross that line.

That's all fine and good, but I have a problem with the drawing of that line—not necessarily in the concept behind it, but in the life application that so often seems to be the result. I don't really think we live in a world that is completely black and white. There are many shades of grey along the road, and the shaded areas end up being slightly different for different people. Nine times out of ten, the line in the sand that we draw for ourselves ends up being in a grey shaded region.

The problem seems to be that a natural result of 'drawing a line' is a life lived as close to that created border as possible. The game becomes how much we can get away with without actually crossing the line. Whether we want to admit it or not, life with a line drawn in the sand becomes a tightrope extravaganza. We pray to God that he'll catch us if we fall over the wrong edge from time to time.

> The game becomes how much we can get away with without actually crossing the line. Whether we want to admit it or not, life with a line drawn in the sand becomes a tight rope extravaganza.

Is this really how you want to live your life? Do you really want to go through life trying to figure out if your particular shade of grey is closer to the black end of the spectrum than the white? No one wakes up one morning and decides to step over to the dark side. With apologies (although not really heartfelt) to those of you who are not Star Wars fans, do you think Darth Vader woke up one morning and decided to walk over to the dark side after a long training within the Force? Of course not. Rather, it was the combination of small choices and bad decisions in the grey regions of his life that caused him to realize one day that he was already on the other side.

I had a friend who I was close to during my teen years. She had some issues, but had given her life over to God and was an amazing testament of God's grace and ability to change us from the inside out. She was a woman full of God-given potential, giftings, and abilities. Although we were close in age, I looked up to her as an example of someone who would make it. She had drawn a line of purity within her own life and was determined not to cross it.

Around the time I was sixteen, she turned her back on that line she had once professed. She left one church and migrated to another that would accept her new lifestyle choice. It hurt my own faith to hear of her decision to leave and choose something that I knew was wrong. But it also caused me to look inward. Our struggles were not the same, but the choices before us were.

I don't believe my friend woke up one day and decided she would skip across the line she had previously drawn. Rather, it was a combination of small choices and bad decisions that led her down a path that ended up far from her original intention. Sadly, only a few years later, she stepped off the merry-go-round of life and chose to fast-track her way into eternity.

The news of her death was very hard on me. It is not for me to guess or to judge the state of a person's heart. I can only imagine that the inner turmoil she went through to decide death was the only option must have been unimaginable. I really grieved for my friend. In the processing of my grief, it also served as a warning for me; anyone could find themselves in the same boat. Every one of us is but a few small, wrong decisions away from a very slippery slope. No matter what our 'slippery slopes' look like, they all lead to separation from God's original intention for our lives. May we never lose sight of this truth.

> **Every one of us is but a few small, wrong decisions away from a very slippery slope. May we never lose sight of this truth.**

So, we draw that line in the sand and we declare that on one side of our line is the realm of holiness and on the other side lies the realm of ungodliness. My question to you is this: why are we trying to stay as close to that line as we possibly can? If that is our mentality, the struggles that we face will be a constant and fierce battle for the rest of our lives. We will never gain victory over thought patterns and habits, and we will live on a never ending roller coaster ride of emotions.

There must be a better way than this.

If the area on either side of our holiness line tends to be shaded with grey, may I offer another suggestion? If we truly want to fulfill God's purpose and calling in our lives—if we truly want to see our God-given potential realized and reached—we must begin living our lives as far away from that line as possible. It is time we decided to stop living in border town.

> *Try to live in peace with everyone, and seek to live a clean and holy life, for those who are not holy will not see the Lord.*
> *~ Hebrews 12:14*

You don't have to live a life of defeat. You don't have to live a life of constant failure. Walking through this process of purity successfully involves more than staying on the right side of your line. It involves taking the necessary steps to get as far away from that line as possible.

You can't stop a freight train on a dime. Move your life away from the line so that if temptation comes at you, you will have the distance you need to get the engine stopped without your life derailing in a place you never wanted it to be.

Part 2: A Battleground

## Dealing With the Duality of Fear...

Danielle and I went to a theatre arts production at a local college a few months ago. The evening consisted of three monologues that were written and performed by graduating students. Although all of them were extremely well done, the last one really impacted me.

The setting was of a girl who was stuck in her chair. The chair controlled and constricted all her movements. No matter what she did in life, there had to be a body part that was touching the chair. She struggled and struggled to break free, but to no avail. The chair was a part of her, and it seemed like she would never break free from it. She tried to come to grips with it, she tried to ignore it, she tried to embrace it, but she could never seem to free herself from it.

Suddenly, through a burst of emotions and a flurry of activity, she was no longer attached to it. She finally had what she had been longing for her entire life—freedom. Now she was able to do whatever she wanted—there were no constraints on the potential she would be able to fulfill. With mixed emotions, however, the vignette closes with eyes that glance longingly back at the chair.

It really spoke to me about this process of living a life of self-sacrifice and purity. We each have habits in our life that we are trying to break free from. We know our tempers, our fantasy lives, and our negative relationship patterns are not healthy. We know they are constraining us from realizing and reaching the God-given potential that each one of us has. But try as we might, we just can't seem to break free from them.

Could it be that the only thing holding us back is our own fear? We fear failing for the thousandth time. We fear that God will not be there this time around to pick us up if we fall down. We fear that the people around us will no longer accept us if they find out what is hidden inside and behind the masks we wear. But is there another fear that we haven't dealt with yet?

Do we fear succeeding?

Ouch. Deep down, this is the one fear that none of us are willing to talk about, and I believe it serves as one of the breaking points on our path to inner purity. We fear succeeding. We fear winning the battle and losing the chains that are around us for the simple fact that they are familiar. Yes, they are wrong. Yes, they are holding us back from reaching our potential. But they are comfortable, and we unknowingly fear the possibility of not having that familiarity and comfort on the other side of purity. And so we continue to struggle and lose because that seems better than winning and letting go.

> **The fear of success is the one fear that none of us are willing to talk about, but it serves as a breaking point on our path to inner purity.**

Stop for a moment. This is the last battle line that I want to talk about before we end this section of the book, and I believe God wants to perform a paradigm shift in our thinking if we will let him. Why do we fear the unknown? Why do we fear letting go?

True abandonment refuses the luxury of asking questions. True worship is worship with abandonment. It's time to face your fear. It's time to let go of the realm of comfort and the luxury of having your questions answered. It's time to face this duality of fear—this fear of both failing and succeeding—and put your trust in one who has been longing to hold your hand since the dawn of time. It's time to take the plunge and freefall into the depths of all that God has for you.

> *Such love has no fear because perfect love expels all fear. If we are afraid...this shows that his love has not been perfected in us.*
>
> ~ 1 John 4:18

Allow God's love to be perfected in you. Be willing to experience it fully. Be willing to let your guard down and let his arms wrap around you. Allow God's love into the deep recesses of your soul and the fear that cripples you will be expelled.

Are you willing to participate in the freefall of a lifetime?
Let his love cause your fear to subside.
Jump.

# Part 3: Standing on Firm Ground

...Do not be afraid. Stand firm and you will see the deliverance the LORD will bring you today.

~Exodus 14:13 (NIV)

Cultivate these things. Immerse yourself in them. The people will all see you mature right before their eyes! Keep a firm grasp on both your character and your teaching. Don't be diverted. Just keep at it. Both you and those who hear you will experience salvation.

~1 Timothy 4:15-16 (MSG)

So let's do it—full of belief, confident that we're presentable inside and out. Let's keep a firm grip on the promises that keep us going. He always keeps his word.

~Hebrews 10:22-23 (MSG)

# Chapter 10: Heart Transplant

No matter how deep the stain of your sins, I can remove it. I can make you as clean as freshly fallen snow. Even if you are stained as red as crimson, I can make you as white as wool.

~Isaiah 1:18b

Who may worship in your sanctuary, Lord? Who may enter your presence on your holy hill? Those who lead blameless lives and do what is right, speaking the truth from sincere hearts.

~Psalm 15:1-2

Wisps of grey hair get blown out of the way of eyes that carry a deep sparkle within them, a sparkle that has survived the passing of countless ages since they first began to shine. The old man's hands are wrinkled with time, worn and callused from the monotony of the day's work. They don't mind, though...these hands enjoy the part they play in the task before them. Their grip becomes a little firmer as a beautiful groove begins to take shape from within a mound of clay. A smile appears on the old man's face. The sparkle in his eye becomes just a bit brighter.

Slowly and painstakingly, the groove takes shape, and the mound of clay begins to take the form of what was birthed in the mind of the old man long before it was ever laid upon the table. This collection of mud—this anthology of rock and dust, sand and water—this lump of nothing is becoming something, giving birth to a masterpiece that only the master could envision.

Life appears from the work of his hands...hard pieces of clay have become soft muscle tissue; jagged rocks have become malleable walls that begin to push life-giving blood in and out of this newly formed pump. A heart has been formed—the life-granting and life-sustaining centre of the master's creation. His work is good and his smile is true. He takes delight in the form before him.

God has placed such a heart within each one of us. It was once as soft and delicate as the one I have just described. The same amount of care, of compassion, and of love was put into the making of yours as well. God knit you together in your mother's womb (Psalm 119:13). He could have snapped his fingers and made you appear, but he wanted to *create* you. He wanted to gently form the masterpiece that had been birthed in his mind long ago. God took the time to shape you, to wire you up with your own personality, and to breathe life into this new creation. His eyes sparkled just a bit brighter the day you came into this world because he saw that his work was good and he took delight in you.

Over time, however, I think many of us have lost the malleability of our once soft and delicate spiritual heart. Just as fat and cholesterol clog up the free flowing pathways of our physical heart, sin and bitterness tend to clog up the flow of our spiritual heart. What was once soft and delicate has become hardened. What was once life-giving has become life-threatening.

> **Over time, many of us have lost the malleability of our once soft and delicate spiritual hearts. What was once life- giving has become life-threatening.**

You've seen the signs. Shortness of breath and numbness on the left side of your body are warnings that you need to get your heart looked at quickly. Why don't we pay such close attention to our spiritual heart? Instead, we allow hurt to take control and clog up our thinking. Depressing and degrading thoughts infiltrate our mind and block the spiritual flow of our life-giving centre while we try to ignore or even deny it. Numbness in our conscience produces acts we would not normally do, and we allow it to happen.

You can ignore the physical signs for a time, but sooner or later you will have to deal with the junk that you have allowed around your heart. Likewise, spiritually, the signs are right in front of us. Yet we labour on this walk of purity—we struggle through the process and seem to gain no ground. Our walk often consists of one step forward and two steps back and we can't figure out what's wrong.

Maybe it's because we have ignored the warning signs of a spiritual heart in danger. Maybe it's time to allow the Potter's hand to do its work once again. Maybe it's time to allow him to break off the hardened pieces that block the flow and to mould and shape you back into his original design.

The truth is, he has always been trying to keep your heart soft. His hand has always been there, trying to guide you along the right path—the path that will keep your life song singing and your spiritual blood flowing. Unfortunately, we shy away from his firm grip. We demand control of our own life, our own destiny, our own way. Being reshaped isn't always the most pleasant feeling, so we choose to ignore the doctor's orders of lifestyle changes while the walls of our arteries and vessels continue to thicken and our spiritual blood struggles more and more to get through.

A key factor to living our lives as a reasonable act of worship is allowing God to keep our heart clean and soft before him. That might involve a bit of a heart transplant from time to time. God is willing to do the operation if we are willing to lay our life in his hands.

> *Then I will sprinkle clean water on you, and you will be clean. Your filth will be washed away, and you will no longer worship idols. And I will give you a new heart with new and right desires, and I will put a new spirit in you. I will take out your stony heart of sin and give you a new, obedient heart. And I will put my Spirit in you so you will obey my laws and do whatever I command.*
>
> *~ Ezekiel 36:25-27*

Living out this process of purity involves allowing God to do a spiritual heart transplant. It requires a willingness to let go of some of those things you have held on to for comfort's sake. It means that you are prepared to be opened up and showcased—to be transparent and vulnerable about the stuff you struggle with and the things you fear. And it means that you are willing to make changes to your lifestyle to become a little more proactive about taking care of that new heart of yours.

> We shy away from his firm grip. We demand control of our own life, our own destiny, our own way. God is willing if you are. Lay your life in his hands.

Your heart is really the most important thing you'll ever own. Allow God to shape it. Allow him to have his way in your life. Listen to him as he gently guides you through this process of purity. Take good care of this heart of yours and be willing to allow the Potter's hand to push and prod, to gently but firmly shape you into the person that he knows you can be: his masterpiece.

The state of our heart is incredibly important to our success in living our lives in purity. We have to go beyond the thoughts and the actions that we have already looked at—we need to be changed deep within.

> But so much more is involved in changing from the inside out than pulling rotten fruit off the tree. Our struggle against sin requires a far tougher battle than the struggle to do right and not do wrong. When the battle is fought by trying hard to do all the Bible commands, eventual defeat is guaranteed. Either we'll slip into defeat and frustration or we'll become stiff and self-righteous in our disciplined conformity to standards, unable to relate deeply to anyone, including God.
>
> ~ Larry Crabb[29]

Change needs to take place from inside of us, from the very core of our being. We will not be able to stand upon firm ground and live out this process of purity unless we allow our hearts to be checked and cleansed daily. Just as there are prescribed steps to taking care of our physical heart, there are also steps for carefully looking after our spiritual heart. These are what we want to look at here.

## LEAVE ME ALONE...

I wear a lot of hats in the run of a day...school teacher, piano teacher, math tutor, worship leader, publisher, writer, leadership trainer, husband. No matter which of these hats I may be wearing at any given moment, I am constantly interacting with people. I love every hat I wear, but to be honest, at the end of the day it's nice to just go home with my wife and not talk to anyone. After all the interaction, the talking and decision-making, it's nice to simply 'veg' and not think about anything.

> Sometimes, I just want to be left alone.

I am sure you have been there as well. You just reach a point where you want to shut your brain off for a while. You simply want to be by yourself. You want to shut out the world around you. You want to forget about life for a moment. Sometimes, you even want to forget about God and shut him out as well. You don't really want to pay attention to the constant care and attention he is asking you to give to your spiritual heart.

> Sometimes...
> Sometimes more than sometimes.

Perhaps this is something we say too often to God in the run of our daily lives. Maybe it's not said in audible words, but I think we often find ourselves expressing the sentiment in our actions. God's hand tries to mould our heart into the soft muscle he designed it to be, but we decide we would rather get off the altar of self-sacrifice and move as far away from that heart transplant as possible.

> **We often find ourselves asking God to leave us alone. We often decide we would rather get off the altar of self-sacrifice and move as far away from that heart transplant as possible.**

The townsfolk from the region of Gadarenes certainly told Jesus how they felt in actual and audible words. You can read of the account in Matthew 8:28-34. Jesus was fresh off the boat from his overnight cruise across the Sea of Galilee when he encountered two men possessed by numerous demons. Jesus took compassion on the men and miraculously healed them by casting the demons out of their lives and into a local pack of pigs. The pigs consequently flew off the handle and over the cliff, causing local bacon sales to go down the drain. But read what happens next...

> *The entire town came out to meet Jesus, but they begged him to go away and leave them alone.*
>
> *~ Matthew 8:34*

Why did they ask to be left alone? Perhaps they were scared of Jesus' power. Perhaps they were angry over their plummeting pork chop stocks. Whatever the reason, Jesus seems to have done what they requested. Chapter nine of Matthew opens up with this phrase, "Jesus climbed into the boat and went back across the lake..."

The thing about God is that he will do what you ask. Whether you say it in word or in deed, if you want to be left alone, he will grant your request. But just as ignoring your cholesterol level will eventually catch up to your physical heart, ignoring the patient pruning of your spiritual heart will lead to decay and defeat.

Looking after our heart is never easy, but always necessary. It involves a consistent effort to get up onto that altar of sacrifice and to let God have his way. The consistency gets tiring and we can be tempted to take a break. We can be tempted to ask God to leave us alone for a time. Ultimately, the choice is ours to make.

One of the things all heart transplant patients have to watch out for in the weeks after surgery is organ rejection. Simply put, the new organ is not welcomed by the body. The immune system of the heart patient considers the transplanted heart to be some sort of infection and actually tries to fight it. In essence, the body doesn't want this new heart it has been given, and it is asking to be left alone.

Are we doing the same spiritually? Spiritual heart surgery is never a painless thing, and there are times when we are tempted to fight against the changes God requires; our old nature tries to reject the new heart we have been given. The difference here is that we can override the urge to reject the spiritual transformation.

In America, patients who have made it to the waiting list for a heart transplant receive a pager. When the pager goes off, it is their cue that a heart has become available and they have a two-hour window to get to the hospital to be prepped for surgery.[30] What goes through a person's mind when they are walking down the grocery isle and their pager goes off? Surely there is excitement. The moment they have been waiting the last several months for has finally arrived. They are given a chance for a new lease on life.

At the same time, I would imagine there are also mixed emotions. I wonder if they consider that someone's death has brought about their chance for new life. Do they have second thoughts about actually going through the process—the complications that could arise, the complete change in lifestyle it will cause, the rehabilitation work that will be involved on the other side of the surgery? Is there a moment of second-guessing as they find their way to the hospital? Is there a time of doubt as they begin all the tests and pre-surgery preparation involved for such a complicated procedure? Will they question if they really want to go through with all of this?

Ultimately, the choice is theirs. They can choose to back out at any given moment before the surgery starts. I don't think that happens much, though. Most realize it is their only hope for regaining a quality of life for their remaining years on earth.

The same is true for you as well. God has paged you, and he is ready to perform a heart transplant on you. Too many times, we opt out of the spiritual surgery because we are too scared of the process. Instead, we politely ask God to leave us alone, allowing our fears to control us.

> **Remember that someone had to die in order for us to receive this new heart. Jesus paid that price with his death on the cross. Are we willing to let that paid ransom be wasted?**

We need to remember, however, that someone had to die in order for us to receive this new heart. Jesus paid that price with his death on the cross so that we might be given a chance to have new life. Are we willing to let that paid ransom be wasted?

If we tell God that we don't want him, the door of our heart then opens up to other things that will try to manipulate and control us. At the end of the day, we are never just left alone—there is always something vying for our attention. The choice is ours. Either we are crucified with Christ, as

Paul says in Galatians 2:20, or we crucify him again by saying we don't want his presence in our lives. Either we nail our own desires to the cross, or we shut him out and serve another master. No matter how you look at it, you are never left alone.

Consider the choice. The pig farmers chose their bacon, Judas chose his own plan, and Peter chose his Messiah. It's not a matter of being left alone but a matter of declaring allegiance. Whose authority will you declare today? Whose will you declare tomorrow? As long as we walk this earth, the choice will be in front of us. We can't run away from the choice, but we can choose to run to God. Choose him. Rely on him when your own strength is gone. Allow him to be your king, and accept the heart that he is offering you.

> Your pager is going off.
> What do you choose?

## This Little Light of Mine...

I performed a heart transplant last night...some people would think that makes the scope of my abilities pretty well-rounded. Actually, it was a virtual surgery on a children's educational website. This one only took about 15 minutes, but I was amazed at the complexity of the surgery. The intricacy and detailing that it involved, even on a children's website, was astounding.

The heart is a very complex organ. Careful study of its design and function must be completed by anyone who is going to specialize in the field. Heart surgeons commit themselves to well over a decade of post secondary education before they ever perform their first operation under an official heart surgeon label. Rightly so. Would you really want a 22-year-old undergraduate with a Bachelor of Science opening up your heart and undertaking such a complicated procedure?

Our spiritual heart is just as intricate and detailed. It is a storehouse for so many of the things that make up the essence of who we are. It is the centre of our being, the life-sustaining core. Within our spiritual heart, we carry information about our past, our hopes and dreams for the future, and even our personality traits. It is truly the essence of our identity.

> Our spiritual heart is a storehouse for so many of the things that make up the essence of who we are. It is the centre of our being, the life-sustaining core.

We often refer to the heart as a house full of rooms. In one room we store memories of past events, in another we store our thoughts and feelings, and in another we store coping mechanisms for our relationships. It really is a simple analogy of a very complex organ. Our physical heart has countless connections within the muscle itself which interact with the rest of the body. The same complexity exists within our spiritual heart.

So, if we try to envision our heart as a house of rooms, we ought to realize that each room is somehow connected to the other. The contents of one room will ultimately affect the contents of the others. If we are going to undergo any surgery on our spiritual heart, it will necessitate someone who understands these complexities. Thankfully, the one performing our surgery is the very one who formed the vessel long ago. He knows our intricacies better than we ourselves know them and he is more than capable of the task at hand.

Dan Hendrican is a song writer and board member of CPM. He wrote what became the title track of CPM's debut CD a few years ago. It speaks of the desire to have God come and do a deep clean-up of our spiritual heart. It speaks of the willingness God longs to find in each one of us:

## Chapter 10: Heart Transplant

> *Put a candle in every room of my heart*
> *Show me all the things I need to give to you*
> *Bright and morning star—I will never, never fear*
> *I can trust you—you are constant, everlasting*[31]

Are you allowing God to light that candle in every room of your heart? We have talked already about the two rooms that serve as the roots of many issues: the room where lack of trust resides and the room where the spirit of demanding dwells. Are you willing to let God go into those rooms and shine his light in them?

Light cuts through darkness. It is rather piercing if you are in a dark room and someone shines a bright flashlight into your eyes. It can cause a little pain, or at least some discomfort. Allowing God's light into these rooms of your heart might give you similar reactions, but it's both necessary and worth it if you truly desire to live out this process of purity in a successful manner.

What about the other rooms of your heart? The room of unforgiveness. The room of painful memories. Have you allowed God entrance into these spaces? Have you consented to the spring cleaning of the rooms labelled *Past Accomplishments* and *Past Failures*? What about the room of your future dreams and visions? That's a hard one to let him into sometimes. Are you willing to put the contents of that room into your Master's hands?

Allow the light of Christ into every place of your heart—every nook and cranny, every small and intricate space. Let him have his way. Let his hand come upon your heart and keep it the soft muscle tissue it was designed to be.

> *Search me, O God, and know my heart;*
> *test me and know my thoughts.*
> *Point out anything in me that offends you,*
> *and lead me along the path of everlasting life.*
> ~ Psalm 139:23-24

King David knew how vital it was to have his heart in tip-top condition. He was willing to allow God to come and do whatever it took to keep his spiritual heart soft and malleable. Are you? We may allow God to do a certain amount of cleaning and pruning, but we don't necessarily give him access to every place in our heart. There always seems to be a couple of rooms that remain off limits to God.

It's time to give him full access.

It's too bad King Asa didn't have this revelation during his lifetime. He was the third King after the nation of Judah split from the nation of Israel. Rehoboam, the first king of the southern division, started off well but soon set up shrines for idol worship and allegiance to foreign gods. Abijah, his predecessor, was not much better. He was considered a wicked king who "committed the same sins as his father before him, and his heart was not right with the LORD his God" (1 Kings 15:3). Then came King Asa...

> *When Abijah died, he was buried in the City of David. Then his son Asa became the next king. There was peace in the land for ten years, for Asa did what was pleasing and good in the sight of the LORD his God. He removed the pagan altars and the shrines. He smashed the sacred pillars and cut down the Asherah poles. He commanded the people of Judah to seek the LORD, the God of their ancestors, and to obey his laws and his commands. Asa also removed*

> the pagan shrines, as well as the incense altars from every one of Judah's towns. So Asa's kingdom enjoyed a period of peace.
>
> ~ 2 Chronicles 14:1-5

It seemed like Asa was willing to allow God back into the life of the kingdom of Judah, and he did a lot of spring clean-up to prove it. God honoured Asa's attempts by providing peace for the first decade of his reign. Unfortunately, however, Asa didn't go all the way.

> Although he did not remove the high places from Israel, Asa's heart was fully committed to the LORD all his life.
>
> ~ 2 Chronicles 15:17 (NIV)

Asa didn't get to those high places. Now don't get me wrong—I am not trying to be hard on the guy. But I think there is a definite lesson for us to look at here as we study the shape of our spiritual hearts. Asa started off on the right foot when it came to leading the people of Judah, but he needed to go all the way if he wanted to reach his full potential. He needed to have ascended those Judean hills and taken down the shrines that were in the high places. Perhaps, had he done so, his forty-one years of reigning would not have ended in war and oppression.

Ninety percent commitment is just not enough. What might have happened to the history of Judah, had Asa been willing to go all the way in his quest for purity? What sort of potential could have been fulfilled if he had allowed God into every area of his kingdom?

What about you? What potential is not being reached in your life right now because of those rooms in your heart where you have not allowed God full access? Will you allow the complete heart surgery that God is requesting, or are you trying to survive on one working artery?

It is important that we take care of every detail if we truly want to see the fulfillment of our God-given potential. Not only do we need to allow God access to the usual rooms of our hearts, we must also be willing to tear down the shrines in the high places and allow him into the places that, up until now, we have only permitted restricted access.

> **What potential is not being reached in your life right now because of those rooms in your heart where you have not allowed God full access?**

What are the high places in our lives that have not been torn down? In the Old Testament, these places represented worship that was given out of order. Some shrines were set up to foreign gods. This represents worship with wrong direction. Other shrines were erected to pay God homage outside of the temple, something that was not allowed. This represents worship with wrong motives.

In our lives, we often have incorrect priority settings and idols of money or things. We can even have ministries for the wrong reasons. Could these be some of the high places in our lives that we have yet to deal with?

Be willing to go deeper—don't be half-hearted when it comes to this quest for purity. Quiet yourself for a probing conversation with your creator. Allow him to search you. Permit him to do his work in your life. Grant him full access to your spiritual heart. See what the master physician can do with his masterpiece.

# Chapter 11:
# Ponderings for the Passage

Teach me how to live, O LORD.
Lead me along the path of honesty, for my
 enemies are waiting for me to fall.

~Psalm 27:11

Gone are the days of the elevator man. The invention of the elevator opened up a world of possibilities for building structure and function. Architects were now able to design buildings that were taller than three and four stories because people would have the ability to take the elevator. With this new innovation came a new job opportunity as well—the elevator operator. Most people my age probably don't even know the job existed, but watch any old movie and you will see the well-dressed elevator man operating the buttons at Macy's.

Sometimes our life feels like that of an elevator man. We spend our days going up and down. We have high moments where we are on fire for God and our walk is easy. Then we seemingly press a button and head downward to a low moment where we wonder if we can make it through successfully.

This is the journey called life. Get used to it.

Now, I hope that last sentence didn't discourage you. We always need to take comfort in the fact that God is going to be with us every step of the way as we live out this process of purity. His desire is to see our spiritual acts of worship bearing fruit. He will be faithful to celebrate with us in the high moments and stand by us through the low moments. This knowledge becomes a wonderful encouragement—it's something to rejoice over!

> *Therefore, since we have been made right in God's sight by faith, we have peace with God*

> *because of what Jesus Christ our Lord has done for us. Because of our faith, Christ has brought us into this place of highest privilege where we now stand, and we confidently and joyfully look forward to sharing in God's glory. We can rejoice, too, when we run into problems and trials, for we know that they are good for us—they help us learn to endure. And endurance develops strength of character in us, and character strengthens our confident expectation of salvation. And this expectation will not disappoint us.*
> ~ Romans 5:1-5a

Did you catch that? The low moments can be beneficial because they build endurance. A runner does the most for his stamina right at the moment when his body longs to stop. Pushing through those points in his training is the very thing that builds the desired endurance.

**The low moments can be beneficial, because they build endurance. The willingness to push on through those low moments will enable you to obtain the results you have been longing for.**

If you are trying to walk through this process of purity with pure motives and good intentions, you have reason to rejoice! Be encouraged and be excited! Be strengthened in your journey. You will not be disappointed! The willingness to push on through those low moments will enable you to obtain the results you have been longing for.

As you read through this book, I hope you are realizing that a life of purity is not simply something you decide to do and then that's it. It takes work—it takes commitment and a little blood, sweat, and tears at times. But with Christ walking beside you, you will make it!

Since beginning this journey together, we have been coming face-to-face with things that many of us didn't really want to confront. However, this confrontation was necessary to walking out this process successfully. Now I want to look at a few things we need to keep in mind as the journey continues.

We have touched on the battles that we encounter—the internal battles of the thoughts in our minds as well as the external battles of our actions and deeds. Your determination, coupled with the grace and strength of God, will allow you to begin seeing more victories than defeats in these areas of your life. Sustained success comes through putting together all of these little pieces we have discussed. There is no single formula for living a life of purity. Rather, the gradual joining of these thoughts, practices, and actions will culminate in success.

Does that mean those low points in our lives where the struggle seems great and failure seems to win will suddenly be no more? In the verse we just read in Romans, it's pretty clear that struggles will still come. It's so comforting, though, to realize that keeping our heart in the sacrifice of worship will not end in disappointment!

There are always going to be battles and trials. The secret to staying on the road of purity, however, is to take it one day at a time. Don't get overwhelmed in your low moments and don't get full of pride in your high moments.

> **The secret is to take it one day at a time. Don't get overwhelmed in your low moments and don't get full of pride in your high moments.**

Each step you take in your life needs to be as thought out as the one before it. It is in those moments of success that your continued and deliberate steps become so important; otherwise, your guard in the areas of purity may begin to slip.

If we want to stand on firm ground, there must be steadfastness in our step. For too long, our life has been lived going up in strength and back down in defeat. Our job as the elevator operator has left us with a sadness in our heart and a sickness in our stomach. The following are a couple of keys to help us get off that elevator and onto a steady course.

## COMPLACENCY COMBAT...

They say you can train a dog to stay on your property without a leash. This shocking method uses a special collar. An electric fence emits a current around the perimeter of your property, and if the dog passes through the current, the collar gives Old Yeller a little shock. Once the dog has been conditioned to stay within the perimeters of your yard, the collar and the electric current are no longer necessary. The dog simply won't try anymore because he associates crossing the property line with an electric shock. In a word, the dog becomes complacent. Our canine friend has accepted the boundaries that have been created for him, and no longer has a desire to expand those boundaries.

Many of us have had a similar and shocking chain around our neck for a long time. Habits have controlled us, tempers have limited us, and sinful desires have dictated the success that we experience. Much like the dog within the electric fence, we feel stuck in a virtual cage. The promised land of purity lies just outside the perimeters we presently sit in. We have tried and failed, tried again, and failed again. Each time, we receive a shock to our system that makes us simply want to stop trying altogether. When we come to believe in Christ, however, the electrical current of our cage is turned off. We are free to leave the old property, but for some reason, we still seem to be living within the boundaries of defeat. Have we become content as we are?

On the flipside, success can be just as dangerous a ground as failure. My electrifying analogy shifts slightly, but the message is still current. We start winning the battle for our mind and experiencing victory. We realize that the collar around our neck no longer has the effect it once had, and we boldly cross into the land of purity. The fight is seemingly easy and we begin to let down our guard. Then we suddenly realize that our fight was easy because we were not being tempted—the key players were simply waiting for the right moment when our guard was low enough to shock us back into our defined pen of sin and struggle.

Both of these scenarios define complacency. The first scenario talks of habitual defeat. The danger here is a hardened heart toward the sin that we are fighting. In essence, we give up the fight and allow the issue to become a part of our life instead of wrestling against it. We become content within the boundaries of our sin because that's easier than breaking free. The second scenario deals with the satisfaction of success. As soon as we begin getting a hold of the truths of God's word and see victory in some of these areas of our lives, this next stage begins. Our complacency shifts to believing we will always have success.

In the words of the chief demon, Screwtape, complacency can be one of the best tactics to successfully derail a Christian in his walk of purity.

> The Christians describe the Enemy as one "without whom Nothing is strong". And Nothing is very strong: strong enough to steal away a man's best years not in sweet sins but in a dreary flickering of the mind over it knows not what and knows not why....But do remember, the only thing that matters is the extent to which you separate the man from the Enemy. It does not matter how small the sins are provided that their cumulative effect is to edge the man away from the Light and out into the Nothing. Murder is no better than cards if cards can do the trick. Indeed the safest road to Hell is the gradual one—the gentle slope, soft underfoot, without sudden turnings, without milestones, without signposts".
>
> ~ C. S. Lewis[32]

If we want to walk consistently on the road of purity, we need to see complacency as another battle line in our fight. Sometimes the danger will lie in the fact that there seems to be no fight needed at all. In these periods, combating complacency is the key. It goes back to the 'not even a hint' principle that we discussed in chapter eight. It is during times of complacency that we may be tempted to allow those 'hints' into our lives. Down the road, we could end up as defeated as when we began.

> **We must face the complacency of believing we will never be free as well as the complacency of believing we will always have success.**

Stay true to the course. Be on guard, even when you feel no need to be. Don't let the monotonous and mundane steal away your potential. Don't let success win you over to self-satisfaction. Winning the invisible battle of complacency will allow you to remain outside the spiritual cages that once held you captive.

## THE POWER OF A PARTNER...

We were never created to walk this life alone. By design, we were destined for relationship. God created us to interact with one another in every aspect of life. Walking on the road of purity should be no different.

> *So we are lying if we say we have fellowship with God but go on living in spiritual darkness. We are not living in the truth. But if we are living in the light of God's presence, just as Christ is, then we have fellowship with each other, and the blood of Jesus, his Son, cleanses us from every sin.*
>
> ~ 1 John 1:6-7

Do you catch the subtle truth here? In his letter to the church, John equated living in the light as having fellowship with one another. Let's take a look at Peterson's paraphrase of this verse from *The Message*.

> *If we claim that we experience a shared life with him and continue to stumble around in the dark, we're obviously lying through our teeth— we're not living what we claim. But if we walk in the light, God himself being the light, we also experience a shared life with one another, as the sacrificed blood of Jesus, God's Son, purges all our sin.*

God has called us to live a shared life with one another. This requires sharing both our successes and our failures. Real relationship with a few close people is what God desires for each one of us. He showed us this relationship model while he walked on earth. Jesus had a group of twelve disciples, but then operated within an inner circle as well— people like Peter and John who he poured his heart out to. He was God, and yet in human form was still willing to be vulnerable with his fellow man. Wow—what an example for us to follow!

> **God has called us to live a shared life with one another. This requires sharing both our successes and our failures.**

It is important that every person has some sort of accountability partner. Whether your struggle is food, pride, fantasy, or temper tantrums, it is important that you have a relationship with someone who you can talk openly to about your struggles, your successes, and your failures. It is important to have someone around you that has permission to speak into your life, even when you don't want to hear it.

This is something we all struggle with. No one wants to take off their mask in front of someone else. Deep down, we are terrified about being real with another person.

> Most of us are terrified to be open with each other, not because we're afraid of hurting or discouraging people, but because we profoundly fear that others will retreat from us. We hate to admit that the people we depend on are simply too weak to stay deeply involved once they face all that we are. We don't want to accept the fact that, since the Fall, no human being has the capacity to love us perfectly.
>
> ~ Larry Crabb[33]

I used to cringe at the idea of accountability. I didn't want to let someone into my life in that way. Despite those feelings, I took a chance and forced myself to be real with people in my life whom I felt I could trust. It was in those moments of vulnerability that I felt the most uncomfortable, yet it was also in those moments that I received the most healing.

When you finally take a mask off in front of someone, the weight of hiding gets lifted from you. That is a huge step in living a pure life. Secret sins are much harder to deal with than sins you have brought into the open with an accountability partner. When sin is in the light, it is exposed. This exposure loosens its grip on your life. This doesn't solve all your problems, but it makes them easier to deal with.

**You were created and called to take this chance. It is in the true fellowship of believers that you will walk in the light and stay in the light.** Here you can combat complacency because you have people in your life who are allowed to speak the truth that sometimes you cannot see.

Don't try to walk alone; let the people God has placed in your life help you. Gather people around you that you will allow to speak directly into you. Be willing to be real with them, then watch your spiritual walk grow and flourish.

## USING ALL THE STRENGTH YOU HAVE...

As we close this chapter, one other partner who is there to help us should be remembered. Unfortunately, this partner is often our last resort instead of our first. Sometimes we get so caught up in trying to win the battle that we forget about our most important ally.

The story has been told of a small boy spending his Saturday morning in a sandbox. [34] He loved to play with his cars and trucks, building roadways and city infrastructures within the sand, guided by the help of his plastic pails and shovels.

On this particular morning, the boy was busy creating a tunnel in the sand for his cars. As the tunnel made its way to the middle of the sandbox, the lad found a large rock in his path. If he wanted to continue his tunnel making, the rock would have to go.

The boy laid down his tools and focused his energy on the obstacle. He pushed with all his might, but to no avail. Beads of sweat formed on his forehead as he directed every muscle into shifting that rock's position. Once in a while, he would have enough strength to move the boulder slightly, only to have it roll back on him. There was nothing he could do to get this boulder out of the way. Tired, sweaty, and full of frustration, the overwhelmed little boy sat in the sand and began to cry.

At that moment, a shadow appeared in front of the boy. The small lad turned around, his eyes full of tears, to face his father who had been watching the vignette unfold through the lens of the living room window.

The father inquired as to the boy's problem. Through eyes veiled with tears and discouragement, the son conveyed his woes to the father. The father bent down in the sandbox so that their eyes met and asked his son why he didn't use all the strength that he had.

Astonished, the son looked back at the father. With a perplexed and forlorn tone he exclaimed that he had used every muscle in his little body. He *had* used all the strength he had! The father gently smiled at his son and corrected him. The son hadn't used all the strength available to him because he hadn't asked his father. The father picked up the boulder and moved it out of the way and then lovingly picked up his son and embraced him.

How many times have we tried to fight our battles simply in our own strength? How many times have we faced defeat because we did not go to our source of sustenance? Never forget that you have a Friend who is closer than a brother and a Father who is strong enough to move the boulders of your life out of the way.

> *My flesh and my heart may fail, but God is the strength of my heart and my portion forever.*
> ~ *Psalm 73:26 (NIV)*

Never forget your most important source of strength. The one who formed you is waiting for you to call on him. The one who shaped you is longing to see your hand extended to him. The one who loves you is anxious for you to ask for help. Will you? You can't live this life successfully in your own strength. Thanks be to God that we have a lot more strength available to us than our own!

*Chapter 11: Ponderings for the Passage*

You can do this. I believe in you, because I believe in the faithfulness of the one who created you. Through the high points and the low points, be encouraged. God is there with you every step of the way as you commit your life to him. Allow him to be the ruler of your heart.

# Chapter 12:
# Are We There Yet?

> But this precious treasure...is held in perishable containers, that is, in our weak bodies....We are pressed on every side by troubles, but we are not crushed and broken. We are perplexed, but we don't give up and quit. We are hunted down, but God never abandons us. We get knocked down, but we get up again and keep going.
>
> ~2 Corinthians 4:7-9

Don't you love road trips? Bags of junk food litter the floor as the vehicle upholstery emits an aroma that can only be described as the smell of a group of people stuck in a car for more than 24 hours. When I was a teen, my youth group loved to do road trips. The best ones involved people piled together and crammed into a 15-passenger van trying to sleep on and over each other at 2:00am. There are many stories (some would not be allowed to be published) that run through my mind about those road trips. Apart from the stories, and regardless of the destination, there was one phrase constantly spoken:

> Are we there yet?

At the end of the day, people want to have a destination. We don't like to be in limbo. When I graduated from university and took a teaching job in Calgary, it involved moving across Canada in a U-Haul. I had the truck booked for eleven days, so I figured I could take my time and do some sight-seeing along the way. But there's something about having your entire life in the back of a truck that makes you want to just get where you are going and unload it. Instead of taking my time and enjoying the land, I was in a hurry to get my new life started. I didn't want to enjoy the process of getting there.

Tim MacDonald knows how to have fun on a road trip. While he was my youth pastor, I sometimes wondered if he enjoyed the road trip more than the event at the final destination. He used the time in limbo to have a little fun, play a few pranks, and build relationships with the group of teens who were stuck with him for the duration of the drive. It's not like they could go anywhere. He made the most of it and got to know them for who they were. The same rings true in our spiritual lives.

> *For this world is not our home; we are looking forward to our city in heaven, which is yet to come.*
>
> *~ Hebrews 13:14*

> *So we are always confident, even though we know that as long as we live in these bodies we are not at home with the Lord. That is why we live by believing and not by seeing. Yes, we are fully confident, and we would rather be away from these bodies, for then we will be at home with the Lord.*
>
> *~ 2 Corinthians 5:6-8*

Our life is a road trip—we have not yet reached the destination for which we have been created. We have been created to live with God in heaven. Right now we are all in a state of limbo that I would like to label *The Road Trip of a Lifetime*. What are you doing with your trip? Are you making the most of it, or are you grumbling in the backseat, simply asking if we are there yet?

We all want to finish this process. We all want to say that we have things under control, that the things that once ensnared us no longer have an effect on us. We all want to declare our arrival at this destination called purity. That's the goal we are working toward—that's the prize at the end of the journey.

When will we be able to declare ourselves 'there'? The Apostle Paul never seemed to reach a point in his life where he could finally state that he had arrived. Throughout his letters, he encourages the church to press on. We have already discussed Paul's 'active' vocabulary in those passages. His encouragement to the Corinthian church quoted at the beginning of this chapter is for us as well.

I sincerely hope that you have been encouraged throughout our journey together. I believe that if we can grasp some of the principles I have outlined in these chapters, we can have a much more successful journey as we walk this road of the process of purity. We must be willing to be real with our God, ourselves, and the people around us.

> We are all on the road trip of a lifetime. Are you making the most of it, or are you grumbling in the backseat, simply asking if we are there yet?

The road trip itself is really not an option. We are here, and we are called to live this life out to the best of our abilities. C. S. Lewis compares it to a compulsory exam:

> Many people are deterred from seriously attempting Christian chastity because they think (before trying) that it is impossible. But when a thing has to be attempted, one must never think about possibility or impossibility. Faced with an optional question in an examination paper, one considers whether one can do it or not: faced with a compulsory question, one must do the best one can. You may get some marks for a very imperfect answer: you will certainly get none for leaving the question alone. Not only in examinations but in war, in mountain climbing, in learning to skate, or swim, or ride a bicycle, even in fastening a stiff collar with cold fingers, people quite often do what seemed impossible before they did it. It is wonderful what you can do when you have to.
>
> We may, indeed, be sure that perfect chastity...will not be attained by any merely human efforts. You must ask for God's help. Even when you have done so, it may seem to you for a long time that no help, or less help than you need, is being

given. Never mind. After each failure, ask forgiveness, pick yourself up, and try again....For however important chastity... may be, this process trains us in habits of the soul which are more important still. It cures our illusions about ourselves and teaches us to depend on God. We learn, on the one hand, that we cannot trust ourselves even in our best moments, and, on the other, that we need not despair even in our worst, for our failures are forgiven. The only fatal thing is to sit down content with anything less than perfection.

~ C. S. Lewis[35]

We cannot be content with anything less than perfection. We must press on and make the most of this road trip of our lives. We need to be willing to do the best we can with the situations we have been given. These are different for each one of us, but the outcome is the same—living out our lives in sacrifice, our reasonable act of worship.

**We need to be willing to do the best we can with the situations we have been given. These are different for each one of us, but the outcome is the same—living out our lives in sacrifice, our reasonable act of worship.**

It's all about the trip. Do you remember that we opened this book talking about the fact that the process is always more important than the product? Well, it's the same here. The journey will be either a good one or a horrible one based on the decisions we make and how much help we enlist from both Holy Spirit and those we have placed around us.

You have before you the road of purity. Your destination, however, is not as important as the trip itself. It is in the process where the growth happens.

You are on the road trip of a lifetime.
What are you doing with it?

## TIME TO ANSWER THE QUESTION…

We are reaching the end of our journey together. This is where many of you are asking how long it takes. When will we be able to say we have conquered the battle and purity is no longer an issue in our lives? When will we be able to say we've arrived?

I remember trying to hash out that question with a close friend. We will never be able to determine ourselves 'there' until we take our last breath and see God face-to-face. Does that mean life will be a constant struggle the whole time we are on this side of eternity? No, I don't believe it has to be—that's why I wrote this book.

> Just as bad habits can be learned
> through repetition and decision making,
> so good habits and godly living
> can be fostered and developed
> through that same repetition and decision making.

We can live pure and godly lives while we walk this earth—it *is* possible! Please hear my encouragement—I believe you can do it! It is our determination to foster and develop good habits and godly living that makes God smile—he delights in our willingness.

The temptations along the way will never go away…it is how we deal with them that counts. An author of a book on purity is not immune to the temptation to get off the road he writes about. A marriage counsellor is not exempt from having an unhealthy fight with his wife. Why? Because these are the natural products of living in a messed up and broken world.

While we will never be able to declare ourselves 'there' until our natural lives on this earth have been completed, it's still something we strive for. We continue to work toward it while we have breath in our lungs and a beat in our hearts.

Saying that we have 'arrived' at any time in our life is a dangerous statement. If we think we have arrived, what are we striving to attain? Hebrews 11:1-2 talks of faith being the substance of things hoped for and the evidence of things not yet seen. We must continually strive to live a life of purity. It will get easier as we train our mind, but to declare ourselves as having arrived before we see our Saviour face-to-face would mean we no longer have anything to hope for. Be aware of this danger.

> **We can live pure and godly lives while we walk this earth—it is possible!**

Taking every thought captive is just as important to the person trying to come off his latest drug-induced high as it is to the man who has been sober for the last forty years. The battle does not end, but the fight becomes easier.

Are we there yet? No, I don't think so. Will we ever be? Yes, I firmly believe so. But the message throughout our journey together has been the message of the process—the small battles and the large battles that we face day in and day out. We can successfully walk this road of purity with God's help and his abundant grace.

We will only be able to declare ourselves 'there' the moment we look into his eyes for the first time. Deep within our soul, we have all been given a desire to hear that one phrase:

> Well done, good and faithful servant.

Well done. Can you hear it? Well done. Can you see him? Nothing else will matter—the questions you are storing up for that day will softly fade away from your mind, meaningless in the light of his face.

If you hear anything from reading this book, please hear this. God loves you. There is nothing you have done and nothing you will ever do to change his love for you. God longs to say those words to you just as much as you long to hear them. Will you let him?

> Well done. Can you hear it? Well done. Can you see him? Nothing else will matter in the light of his face.

God wants to walk this journey with you. He desires to take you by the hand and guide you every step of the way. He doesn't want you to try to accomplish it on your own strength because he knows you can't. Let him take this road trip with you. Let him be your source of strength. A life of purity is attainable if you walk through the process with God as your guide.

## THE REST IS WAITING TO BE WRITTEN...

We have dealt with a lot in this book, and I have enjoyed the journey. I hope that you have begun to see the value in the process—the gem of living our lives out in true sacrifice. Worship is not something that we do on a Sunday morning when we go to church—worship is how we live our lives each and every day. Worship is found in the choices we make from the time we get up in the morning until we go to bed at night. The daily decisions we make, the choice between mounting the altar or going our own way, culminate in what our life of worship looks like.

We have obtained a firm footing by digging deeper into what living a life of purity means and what areas of compromise we need to watch out for. We have been encouraged to take an honest look at ourselves in the mirror, and then to learn to see how God looks at us. We have looked at the importance of sincerity toward both God and man. We have come to realize what true devotion looks like and that it is one of the first steps to the inner change required for pure living. Recognizing where our devotion truly lies is crucial.

> Worship is found in the choices we make from the time we get up in the morning until we go to bed at night. The daily decisions we make culminate in what our life of worship looks like.

Once we established ourselves on firm ground, we looked at the battlegrounds before each and every one of us. From Paul's theology we got an understanding of the battle and the danger of the pendulum swinging too far toward fear or toward grace. We looked at what true sacrifice was all about—how we need to mount our altars and allow God to do the work that he longs to do. Then we looked at the front line of battle—the thoughts of our mind. If we win the battles in this first area, the road of purity becomes a much easier one to walk.

With the front line of battle dealt with, we looked at several other battle lines we must watch out for. We realized the importance of a willingness to get to the roots of the issues in our lives. Getting to the root enables us to understand the triggers that make the battle more difficult. We dealt with having 'not even a hint' of impurity within, starving the sinful nature of our heart. We also looked at dealing with the duality of fear—both the fear of failure and the fear of success within our lives.

Finally, we began to look at how to stand on firm ground once the battle lines have been drawn. We first took a close look at our heart. We need to allow the creator of our heart to mould it into the soft and delicate muscle that he desires it to be. We need to allow God into each room of our spiritual heart—to clean it up and keep it operating the way it should. We touched on the importance of battling complacency in our lives and how essential it is to have people around us for accountability. And we reminded ourselves of our ultimate source of strength—the creator who longs for us to ask him for help.

Now we come to the end of our journey together. However, the end of our journey is really just the beginning. The remaining chapters on our walk of purity are waiting to be written. You are the one who gets to continue this story. You are the one now called to put pen to paper and begin writing.

We started this journey with God's commission to Isaiah:

*Whom should I send...Who will go for us?*
*~ Isaiah 6:8b*

We close with the same call. God is crying out for people who are willing to walk through the process. Are you prepared to answer that call? Remember, God is not asking you to change the world. He is asking you to change yourself. Will you be that change?

A life of purity is our reasonable act of worship.
Are you willing to offer it?

God wants to hear your heart—the good and the bad. He desires to see your transparency. He longs for you to continue this walk with him by your side. What an amazing thought! I want to encourage you to continue your story with him.

What gets written on the rest of these pages is now up to you. What will your story look like? Don't worry about the pages you have filled out in the past—God's grace and forgiveness will be there if you ask him to rule and reign in your life.

God wants to see you walk this walk successfully. The

> **You are the one who gets to continue this story. God is not asking you to change the world. He is asking you to change yourself. Will you be that change?**

creator of the universe is rooting for you! He *will* be with you, every step of the way. Don't ever doubt his presence in your life. Concentrate on the blank page that is now before you. What are you willing to put there? What are you longing to write there?

With God's help, you can make this process of purity truly a road trip of a lifetime, one step at a time. It will be the act of worship that he delights in. I believe you can do it, with all my heart. Don't allow yourself to be discouraged. Draw on the strength of the one who is your complete source. Enjoy life—take pleasure in the road trip that is before you. Have fun on the journey that you were created and destined to have.

You are now the author of the rest of this book.
What will you write?

# Endnotes:

1 C. S. Lewis, *The Four Loves*. © C. S. Lewis Pte Ltd 1960; reprinted with permission.

2 Merriam-Webster Online: http://merriam-webster.com/dictionary/integrity.

3 Geoff Moore/Steven Curtis Chapman, "*If You Could See What I See.*" Copyright © 1993 Sparrow Song (BMI) Peach Hill Songs (BMI) Songs On The Forefront (SESAC) (adm. by EMI CMG Publishing). International Copyright Secured. All rights reserved. Used by permission.

4 This phrase appears in both the Old Testament (1 Sam 13:14) and the New Testament (Acts 13:22).

5 Merriam-Webster Online: http://merriam-webster.com/dictionary/sincere.

6 Saint Teresa of Lisieux, "To Live of Love", (25 February 1895). Translated by S L Emery: http://www.catholic-forum.com/saints/stto2015.htm.

7 C. S. Lewis, *The Lion, The Witch, and the Wardrobe.* © C. S. Lewis Pte Ltd 1950; reprinted with permission.

8 C. S. Lewis, *The Lion, The Witch, and the Wardrobe.* © C. S. Lewis Pte Ltd 1950; reprinted with permission. The actual quote from the book reads as follows:

> "Then he isn't safe?"said Lucy.
>
> "Safe?" said Mr. Beaver. "Don't you hear what Mrs. Beaver tells you? Who said anything about safe? 'Course he isn't safe. But he's good."

9 See both biblical accounts found in Matthew 26:6-13 and John 12:1-11.

10 Larry Crabb, *Inside Out*. (NAVPRESS, 1988), 20.

11 C. S. Lewis, *Mere Christianity*. © C. S. Lewis Pte Ltd 1942, 1943, 1944, 1952; reprinted with permission.

12 Larry Crabb, *Inside Out*. (NAVPRESS, 1988), 18.

[13] John Wyeth & Robert Robinson, "*Come Thou Fount of Every Blessing*" (public domain, CCLI Song 108389)

[14] Check out the whole story in Acts 5.

[15] Larry Crabb, *Inside Out*. (NAVPRESS, 1988), 66-67.

[16] This story is a paraphrase of one found on the net. There does not seem to be a known copyright or author to this story. It can be found on several sites on the web:

http://www.motivateus.com/stories/pearls.htm
http://www.storybin.com/sponsor/sponsor122.shtml

[17] See Exodus 27:1.

[18] Kimberly Hahn, *Life Giving Love: Embracing God's Beautiful Design for Marriage*. (Servant Publications, 2001), 122.

[19] C. S. Lewis, *The Screwtape Letters*. © C. S. Lewis Pte Ltd 1942; reprinted with permission.

[20] C. S. Lewis, *The Screwtape Letters*. © C. S. Lewis Pte Ltd 1942; reprinted with permission.

[21] J.A.B. van Buitenen, *Tales of Anceint India*, 50-51. Copyright © 1959 by the University of Chicago. All Rights Reserved. As quoted in: Henri Nouwen, *The Wounded Healer*. (Doubleday, 1972), 5-6.

[22] Henry Ford, found online: http://www.brainyquote.com/quotes/quotes/h/henryford122817.html.

[23] Saint Augustine, found online: http://www.brainyquote.com/quotes/quotes/s/saintaugus107689.html.

[24] Oswald Chambers, *My Utmost for His Highest*. (April 28); Used by kind permission of Oswald Chambers Publications Association Limited.

[25] Larry Crabb, *Inside Out*. (NAVPRESS, 1988), 160.

[26] The metaphor of the cup and dish used here comes from an analogy Jesus gave to the Pharisees. Check out Matthew 23:26, and surrounding verses for more information.

[27] Oswald Chambers, *My Utmost for His Highest*. (Sept 14); Used by kind permission of Oswald Chambers Publications Association Limited.

[28] Read the full account in Genesis 39.
[29] Larry Crabb, *Inside Out*. (NAVPRESS, 1988), 124.
[30] *Circulation*. 2002;106:1750; © 2002 American Heart Association, Inc. http://circ.ahajournals.org/cgi/content/full/106/14/1750.
[31] Dan Hendrican, *Light of Love*. (CPM Publications, 2000).
[32] C. S. Lewis, *The Screwtape Letters*. © C. S. Lewis Pte Ltd 1942; reprinted with permission.
[33] Larry Crabb, *Inside Out*. (NAVPRESS, 1988), 74.
[34] The following story is a paraphrase of one that I found on the net. The original story is entitled "The Sandbox." The author and copyright of the story is unknown, but the context can be found in several places on the web:

http://my.homewithgod.com/mkcathy/inspirational2/sandbox.html
http://www.storybin.com/builders/builders117.shtml

[35] C. S. Lewis, *Mere Christianity*. © C. S. Lewis Pte Ltd 1942, 1943, 1944, 1952; reprinted with permission.

www.ingramcontent.com/pod-product-compliance
Lightning Source LLC
Chambersburg PA
CBHW060528100426
42743CB00009B/1462